BIG NOTE PIANO LEVEL 2

Arranged by RICHARD BRADLEY

Project Manager: Zobeida Pérez
Art Design: Lisa Greene Mane

BRADLEY™ is a trademark of Warner Bros. Publications

© 2003 BRADLEY PUBLICATIONS
All Rights Assigned to and Controlled by WARNER BROS. PUBLICATIONS U.S. INC.,
15800 N.W. 48th Avenue, Miami FL 33014

Any duplication, adaptation or arrangement of the compositions
contained in this collection requires the written consent of the Publisher.
No part of this book may be photocopied or reproduced in any way without permission.
Unauthorized uses are an infringement of the U.S. Copyright Act and are punishable by law.

RICHARD BRADLEY is one of the world's best-known and best-selling arrangers of piano music for print. His success can be attributed to years of experience as a teacher and his understanding of students' and players' needs. His innovative piano methods for adults (*Bradley's How to Play Piano* – Adult Books 1, 2, and 3) and kids (*Bradley for Kids* – Red, Blue, and Green Series) not only teach the instrument, but they also teach musicianship each step of the way.

Originally from the Chicago area, Richard completed his undergraduate and graduate work at the Chicago Conservatory of Music and Roosevelt University. After college, Richard became a print arranger for Hansen Publications and later became music director of Columbia Pictures Publications. In 1977, he co-founded his own publishing company, Bradley Publications, which is now exclusively distributed worldwide by Warner Bros. Publications.

Richard is equally well known for his piano workshops, clinics, and teacher training seminars. He was a panelist for the first and second Keyboard Teachers' National Video Conferences, which were attended by more than 20,000 piano teachers throughout the United States.

The home video version of his adult teaching method, *How to Play Piano With Richard Bradley*, was nominated for an American Video Award as Best Music Instruction Video, and, with sales climbing each year since its release, it has brought thousands of adults to—or back to—piano lessons. Still, Richard advises, "The video can only get an adult started and show them what they can do. As they advance, all students need direct input from an accomplished teacher."

Additional Richard Bradley videos aimed at other than the beginning pianist include *How to Play Blues Piano* and *How to Play Jazz Piano*. As a frequent television talk show guest on the subject of music education, Richard's many appearances include "Hour Magazine" with Gary Collins, "The Today Show," and "Mother's Day" with former "Good Morning America" host Joan Lunden, as well as dozens of local shows.

CONTENTS

- All I Want for Christmas Is My Two Front Teeth 7
- Deck the Halls 14
- The First Noel 54
- Frosty the Snowman 10
- Fum, Fum, Fum 64
- Go Tell It on the Mountain 49
- Hark! The Herald Angels Sing 52
- Have Yourself a Merry Little Christmas 21
- (There's No Place Like) Home for the Holidays 78
- I'll Be Home for Christmas 70
- It's the Most Wonderful Time of the Year 72
- Jingle Bells 28
- Jingle-Bell Rock 66
- Jolly Old Saint Nicholas 4
- Joy to the World 16
- Let It Snow! Let It Snow! Let It Snow! 40
- The Little Drummer Boy 18
- Nuttin' for Christmas 58
- O Christmas Tree 34
- Pat-a-Pan 62
- Santa Claus Is Comin' to Town 56
- Sleigh Ride 24
- Suzy Snowflake 46
- The Twelve Days of Christmas 36
- Ukrainian Bell Carol 31
- We Wish You a Merry Christmas 76
- Winter Wonderland 43

JOLLY OLD SAINT NICHOLAS

TRADITIONAL
Arranged by Richard Bradley

ALL I WANT FOR CHRISTMAS IS MY TWO FRONT TEETH

Words and Music by
DON GARDNER
Arranged by Richard Bradley

All I Want for Christmas Is My Two Front Teeth - 3 - 1

© 1946, 1947 WARNER BROS. INC.
Copyright Renewed
All Rights Reserved

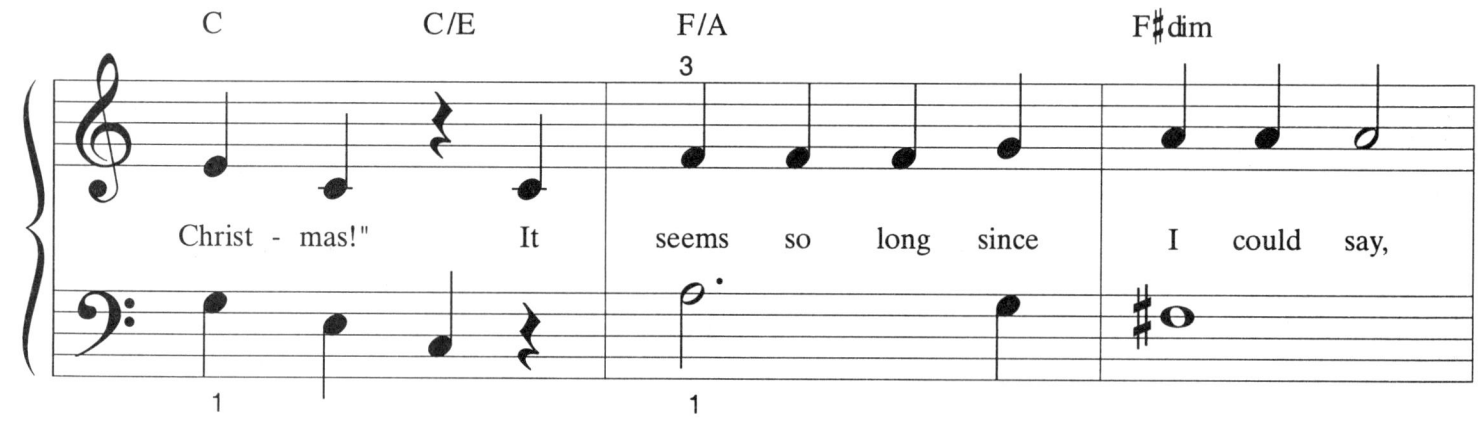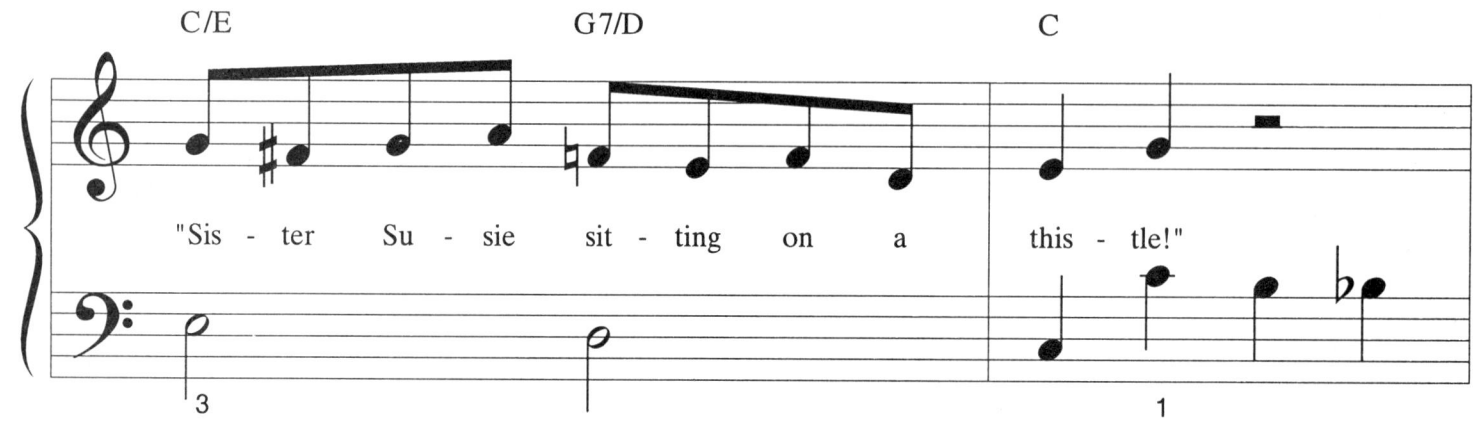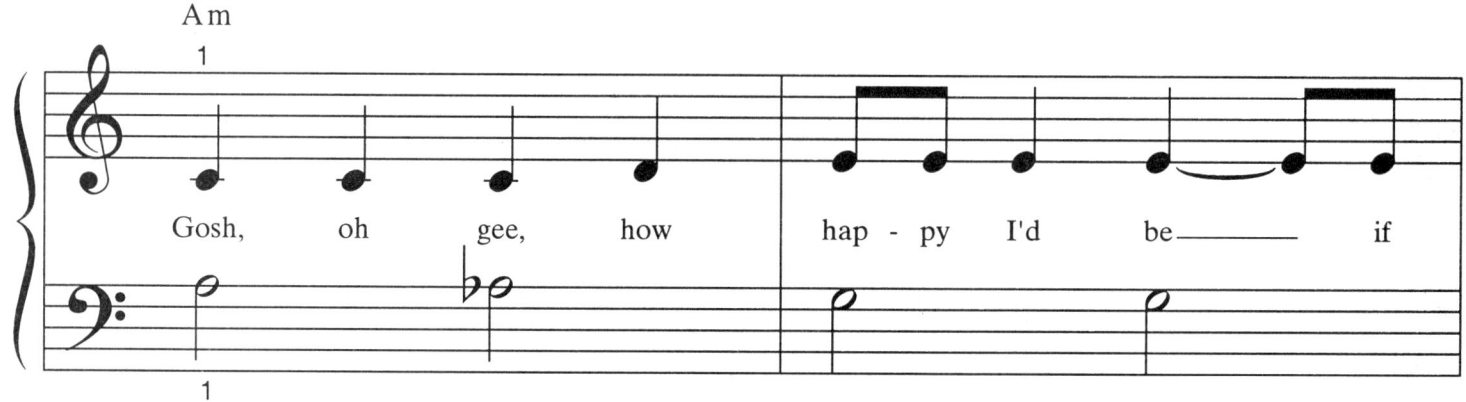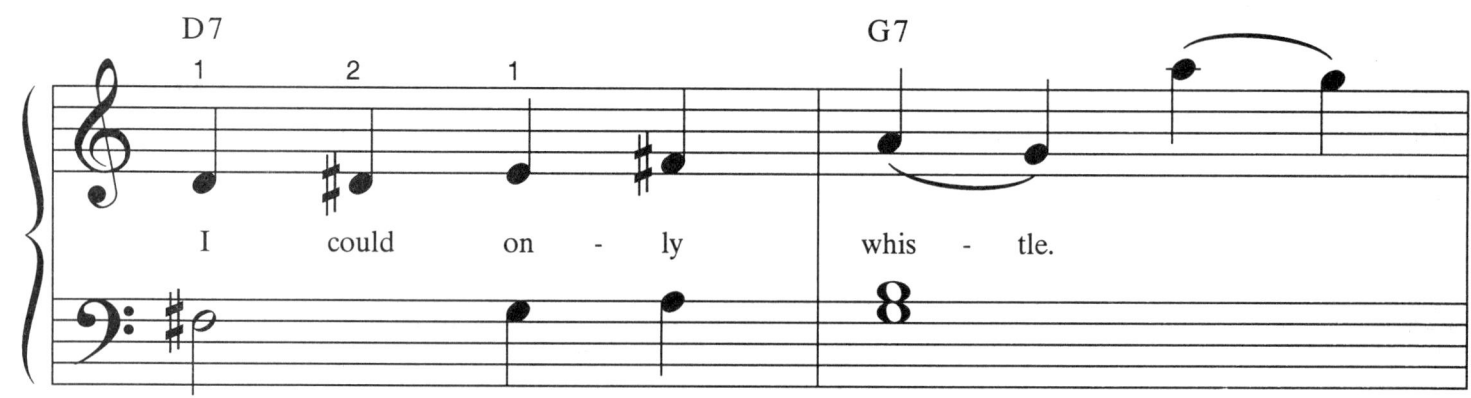

FROSTY THE SNOWMAN

Words and Music by
STEVE NELSON and JACK ROLLINS
Arranged by Richard Bradley

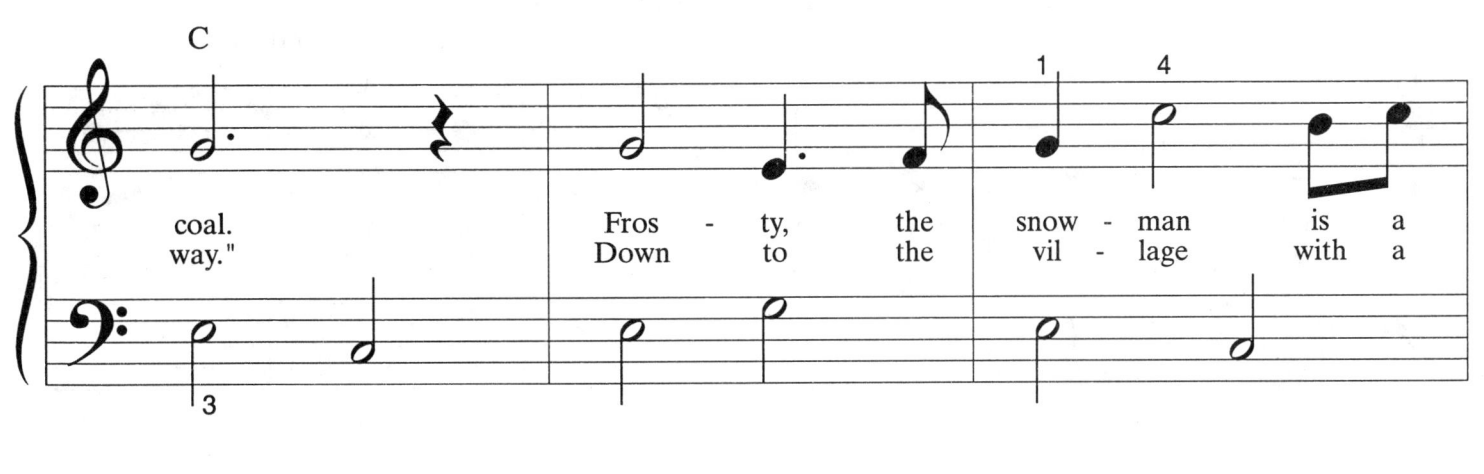

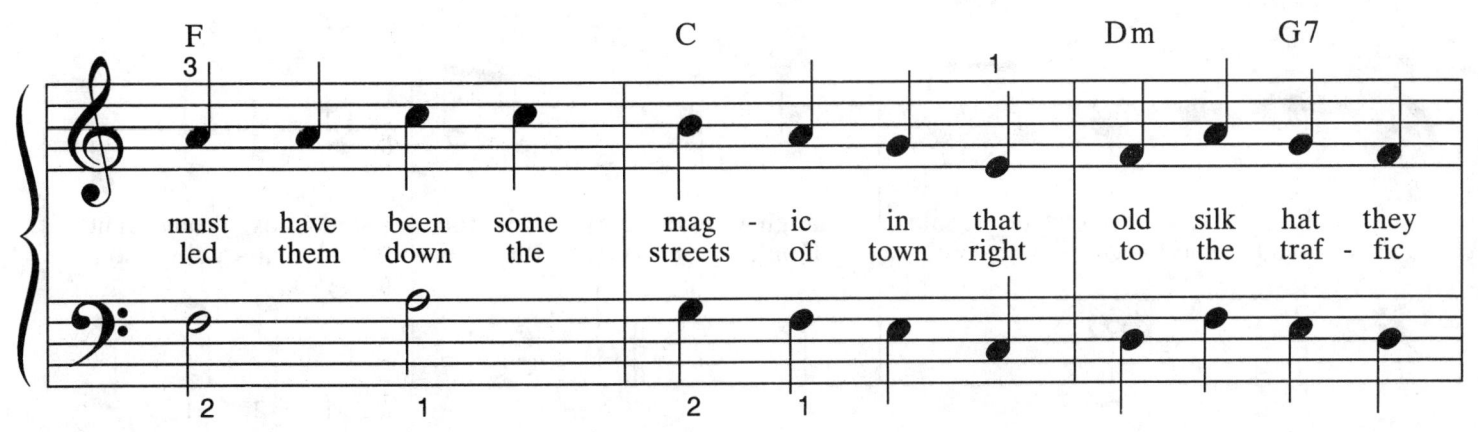

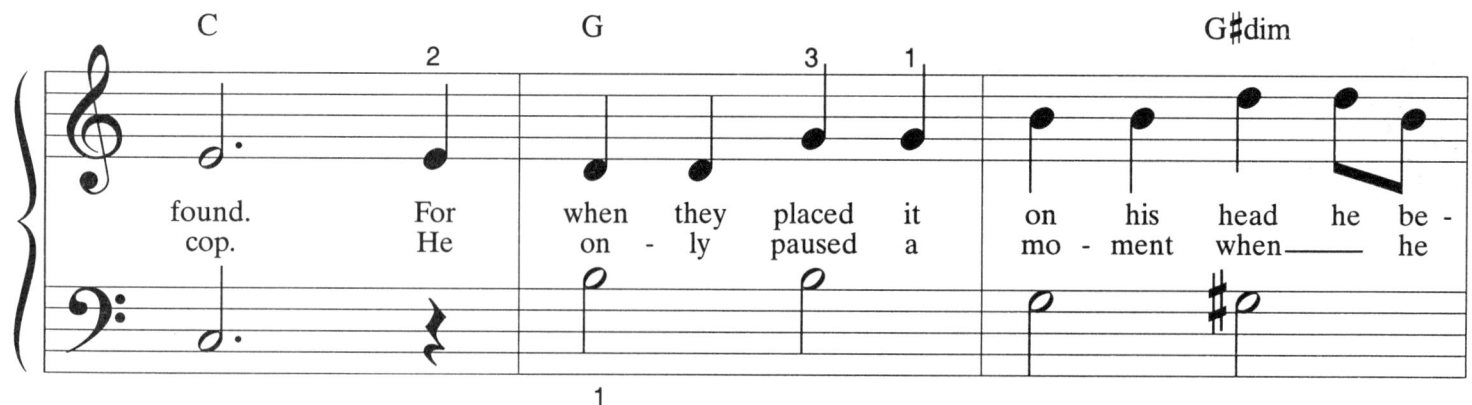

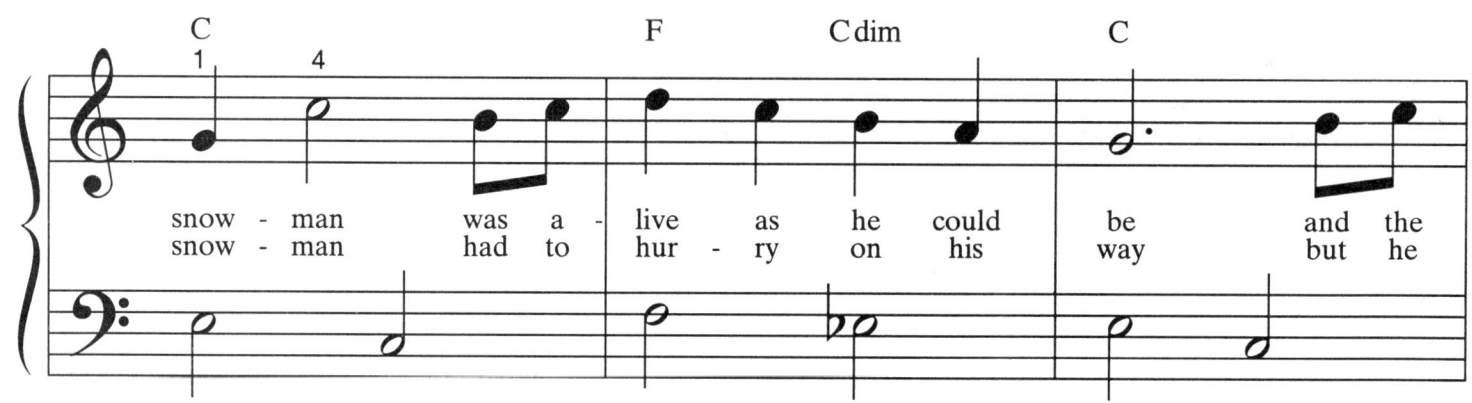

DECK THE HALLS

TRADITIONAL
Arranged by Richard Bradley

JOY TO THE WORLD

By
ISSAC WATTS and G.F. HANDEL
Arranged by Richard Bradley

Joy to the World - 2 - 1

© 1994 BRADLEY PUBLICATIONS
All Rights Assigned to and Controlled by BEAM ME UP MUSIC (ASCAP),
c/o WARNER BROS. PUBLICATIONS U.S. INC., 15800 N.W. 48th Avenue, Miami, FL 33014
All Rights Reserved

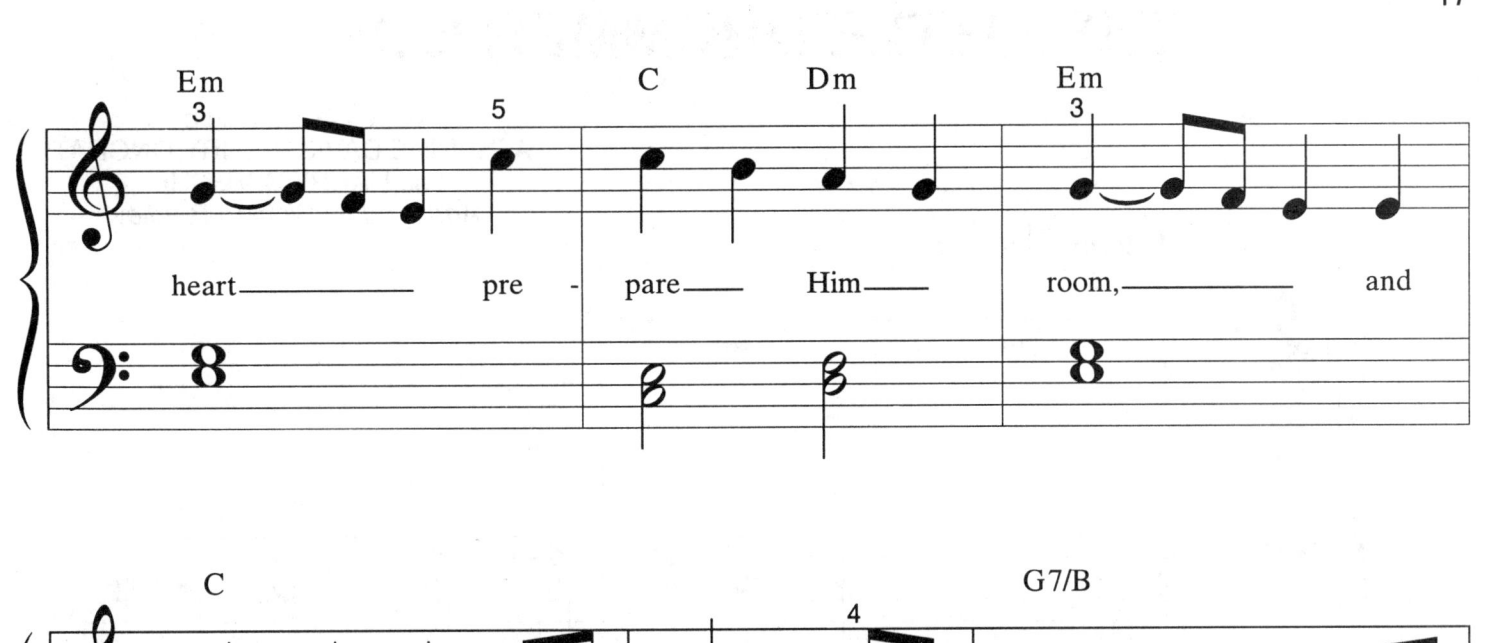

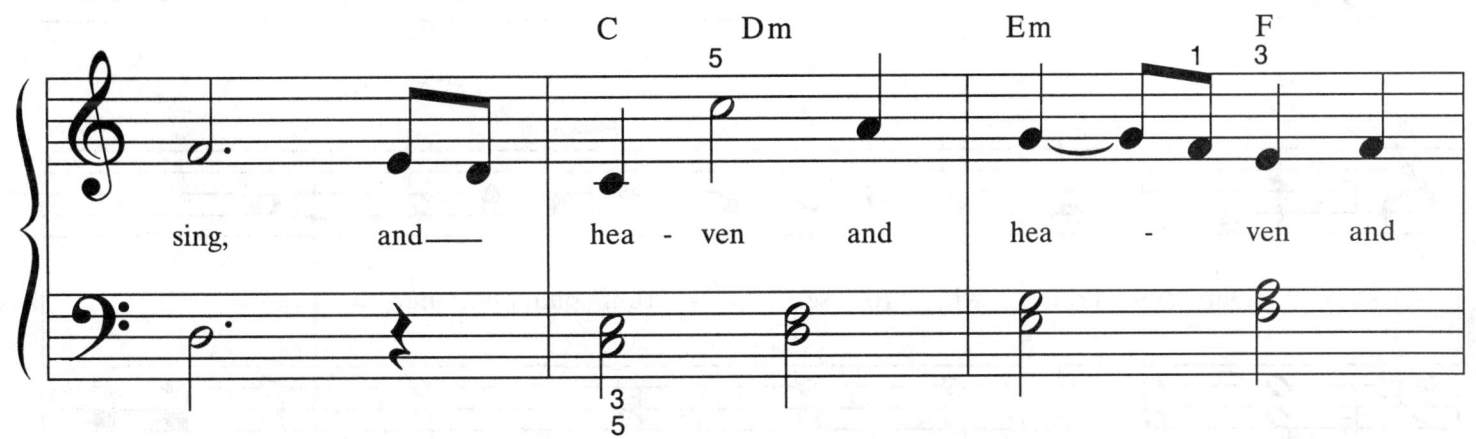
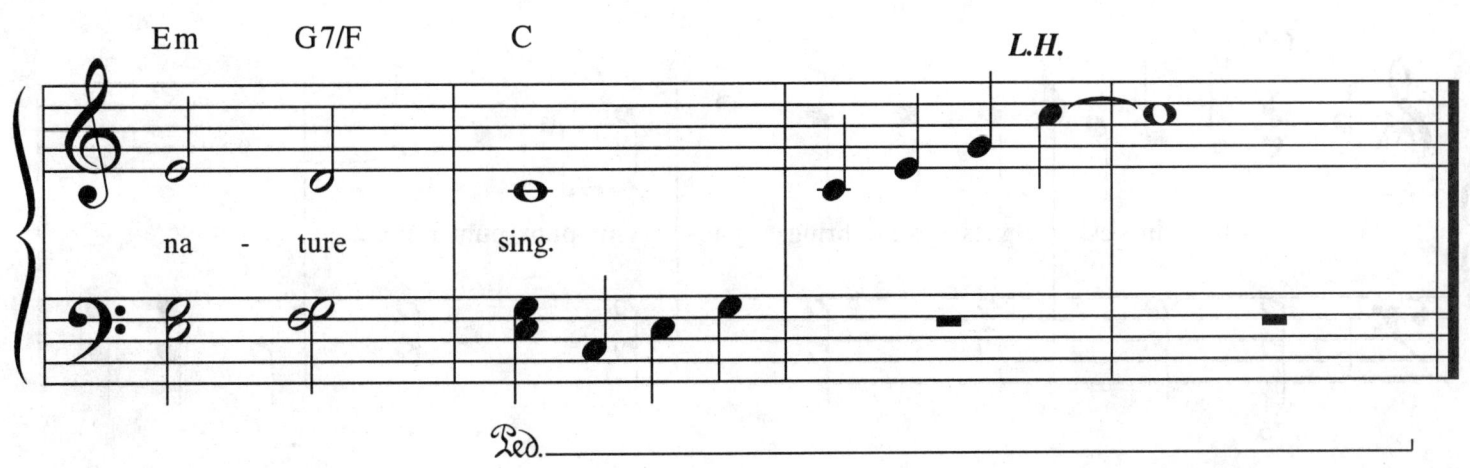

THE LITTLE DRUMMER BOY

Words and Music by
KATHERINE DAVIS, HENRY ONORATI
and HARRY SIMEONE
Arranged by Richard Bradley

Moderate ♩ = 132

Come they told me, pa - rum pum pum pum,

Our new born King to see, pa - rum pum pum pum,

Our fin - est gifts we bring, pa - rum pum pum pum,

The Little Drummer Boy - 3 - 1

© 1958 (Renewed 1986) EMI Mills Music, Inc. and INTERNATIONAL KORWIN CORP.
Wordwide Print Rights on behalf of EMI MILLS MUSIC, INC. Administered by WARNER BROS. PUBLICATIONS U.S. INC.
All Rights Reserved

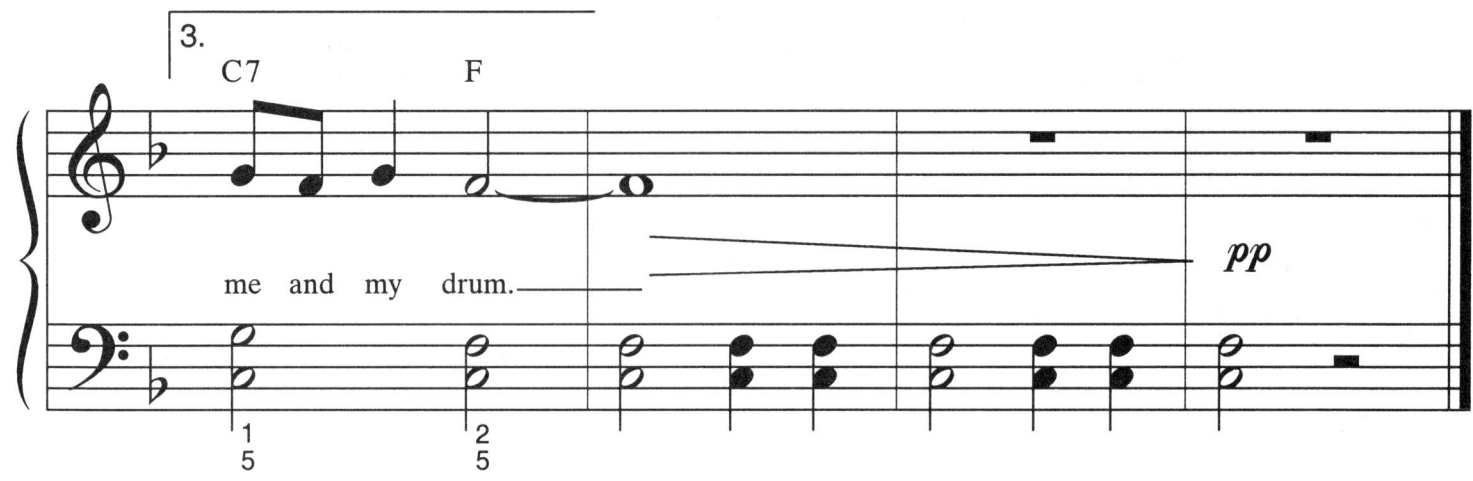

Verse 2:
Baby Jesu, pa-rum pum pum pum,
I am a poor boy too, pa-rum pum pum pum,
I have no gift to bring, pa-rum pum pum pum,
That's fit to give our King, pa-rum pum pum pum,
Rum pum pum pum, rum pum pum pum,
Shall I play for you, pa-rum pum pum pum,
On my drum?

Verse 3:
Mary nodded, pa-rum pum pum pum,
The Ox and Lamb kept time, pa-rum pum pum pum,
I played my drum for Him, pa-rum pum pum pum,
I played my best for Him, pa-rum pum pum pum,
Rum pum pum pum, rum pum pum pum.
Then He smiled at me, pa-rum pum pum pum,
Me and my drum.

HAVE YOURSELF A MERRY LITTLE CHRISTMAS

Words and Music by
HUGH MARTIN and RALPH BLANE
Arranged by Richard Bradley

Dm7 G7 C Am Dm7 E7
gay, from now on, our troub - les will be miles a -
Am C7 F Fm
way. Here we are as in
C Cdim Dm7 G+ C Am7
old - en days, hap - py gold - en days of yore.
F♯m7 B7 Em G+ G D7
Faith - ful friends who are dear to us gath - er near to us once

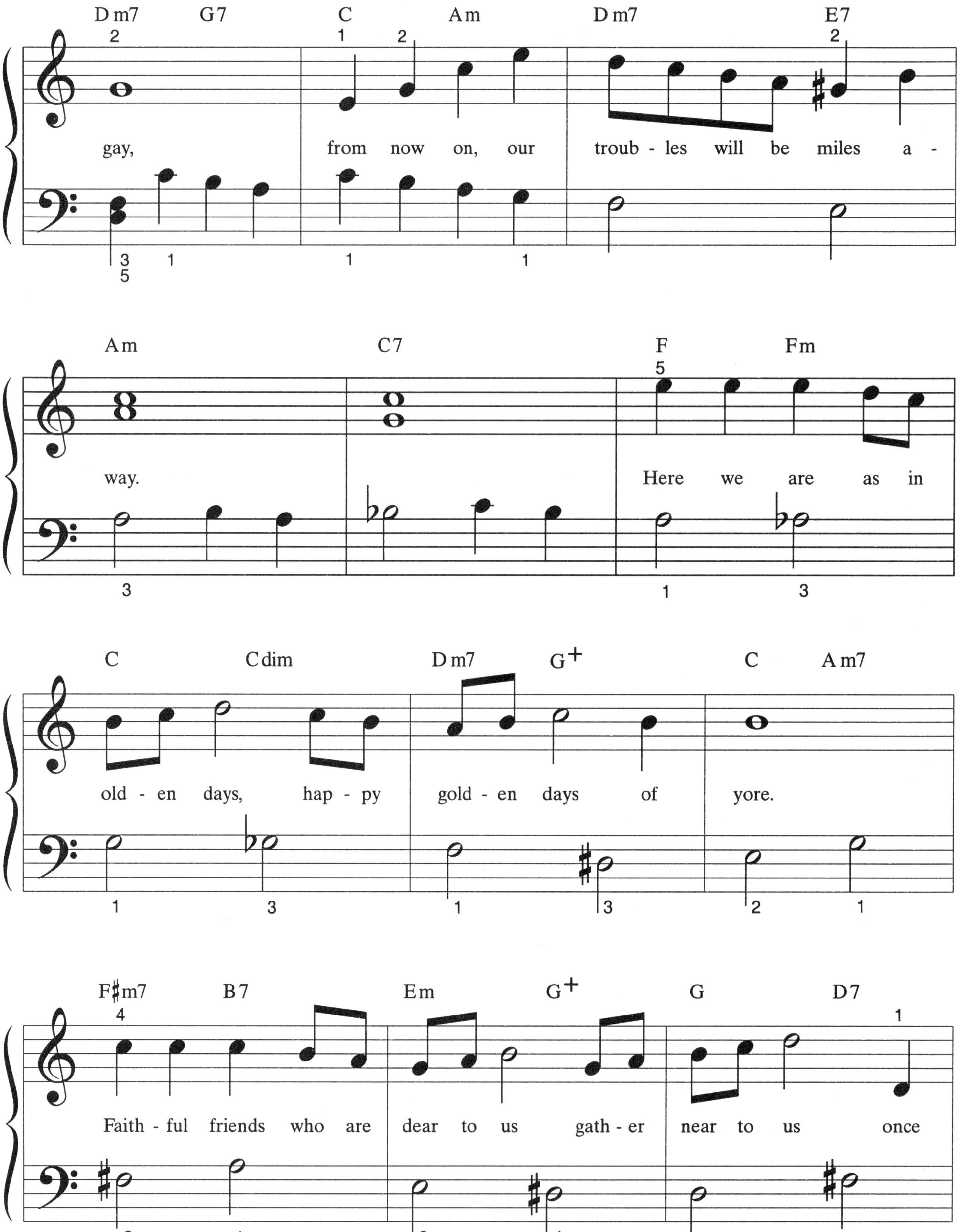

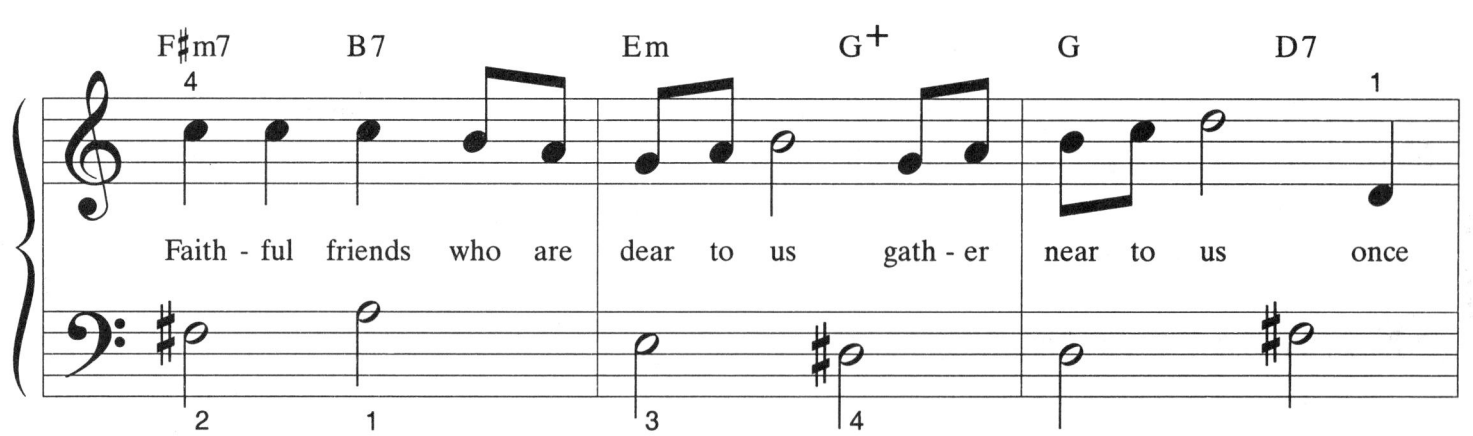

Dm7 G7 C Dm7 G7
more. Through the years we all will be to - geth - er,
C Dm7 G7 C Am7
if the Fates al - low. Hang a shin - ing
Dm7 E7 Am C7
star up - on the high - est bough, and
F Am Dm7 G7 C
have your - self a mer - ry lit - tle Christ - mas now.

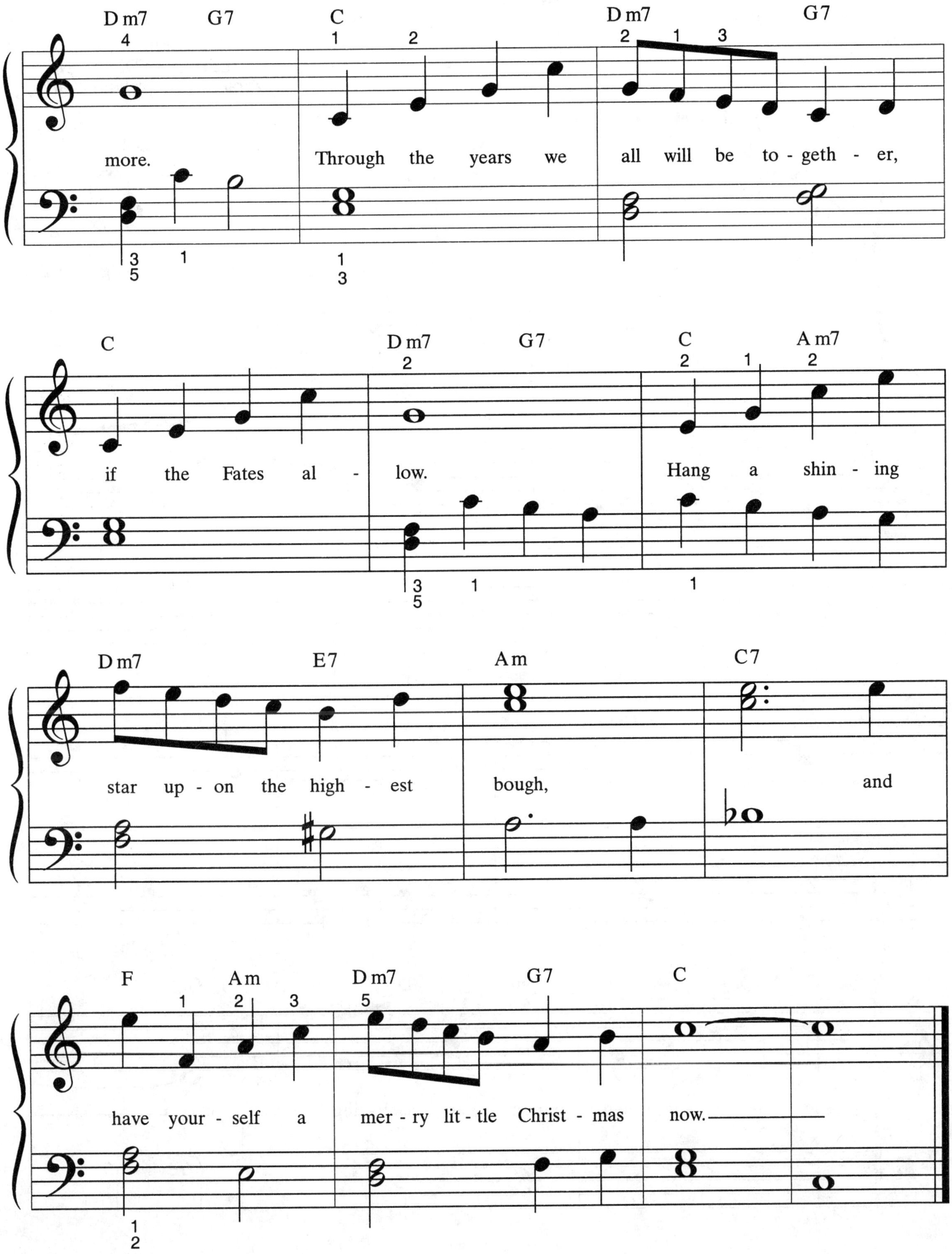

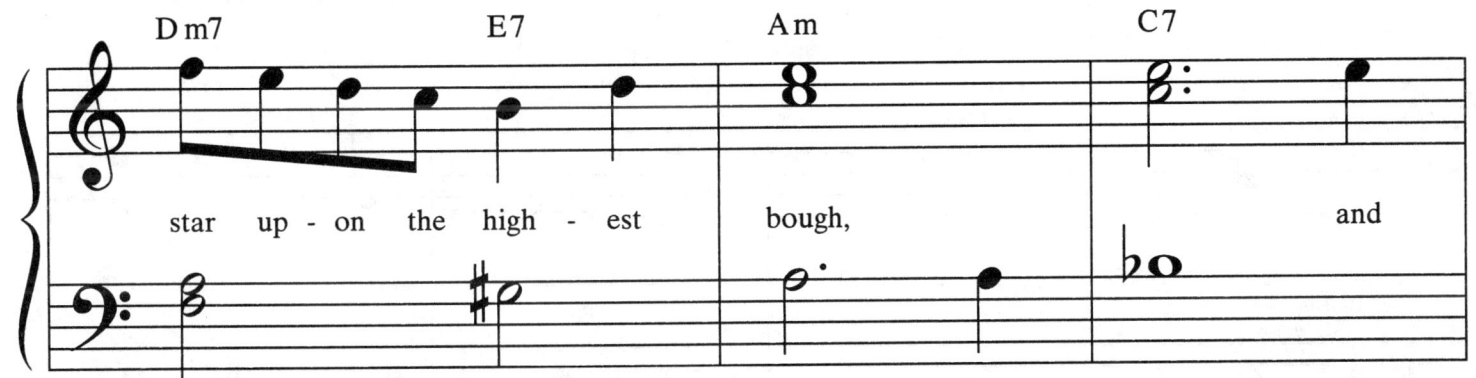

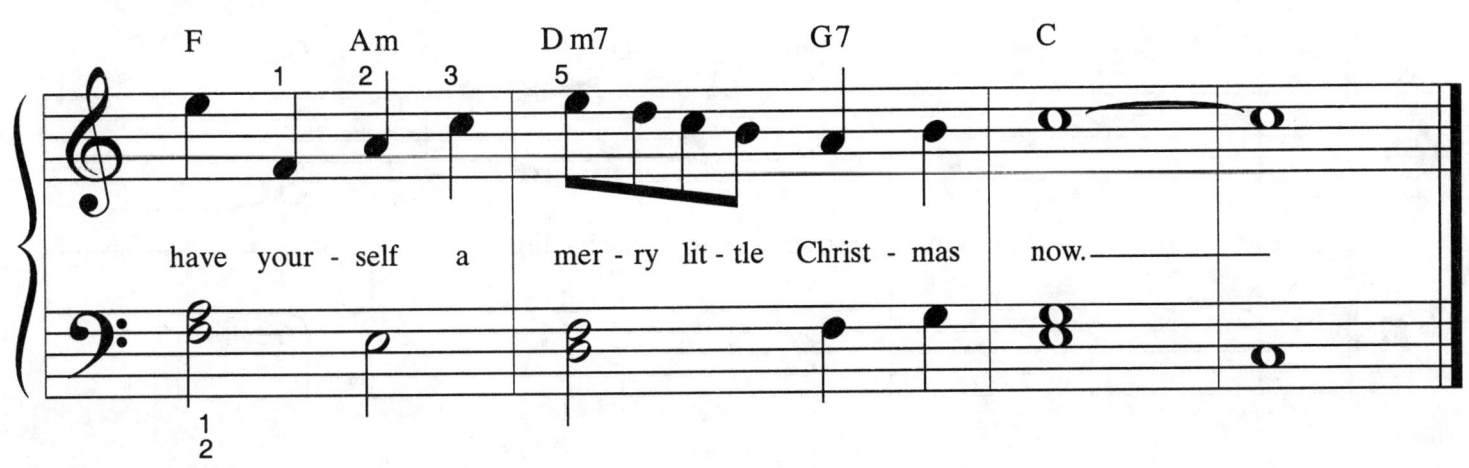

SLEIGH RIDE

Words by MITCHELL PARISH

Music by LEROY ANDERSON
Arranged by Richard Bradley

Sleigh Ride - 4 - 1

© 1948, 1950 (Renewed 1976, 1978) EMI MILLS MUSIC, INC.
Print Rights on behalf of EMI MILLS MUSIC, INC. Administered by WARNER BROS. PUBLICATIONS U.S. INC.
All Rights Reserved

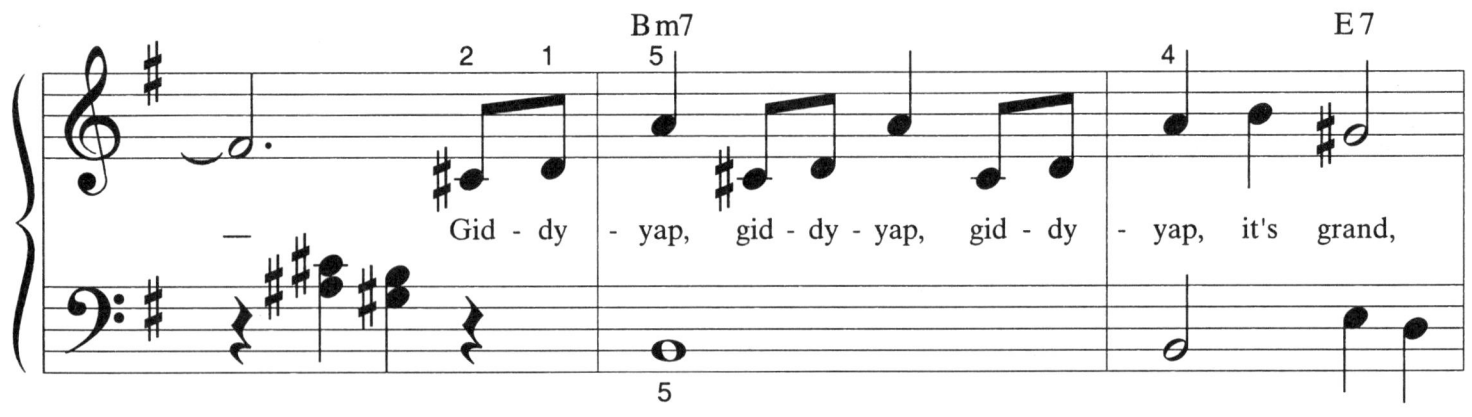

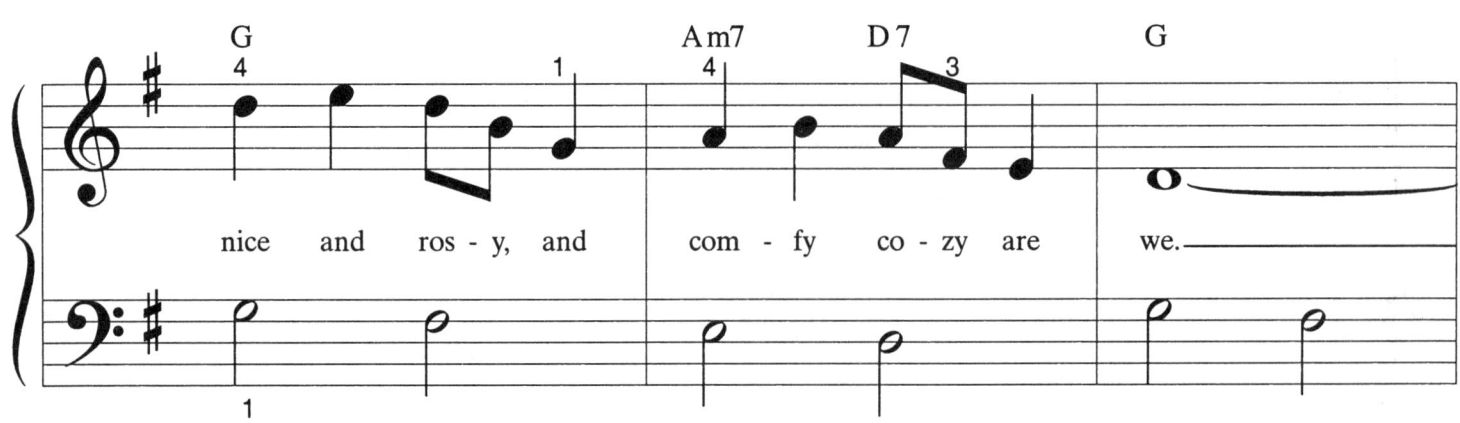

JINGLE BELLS

Words and Music by
J. PIERPONT
Arranged by Richard Bradley

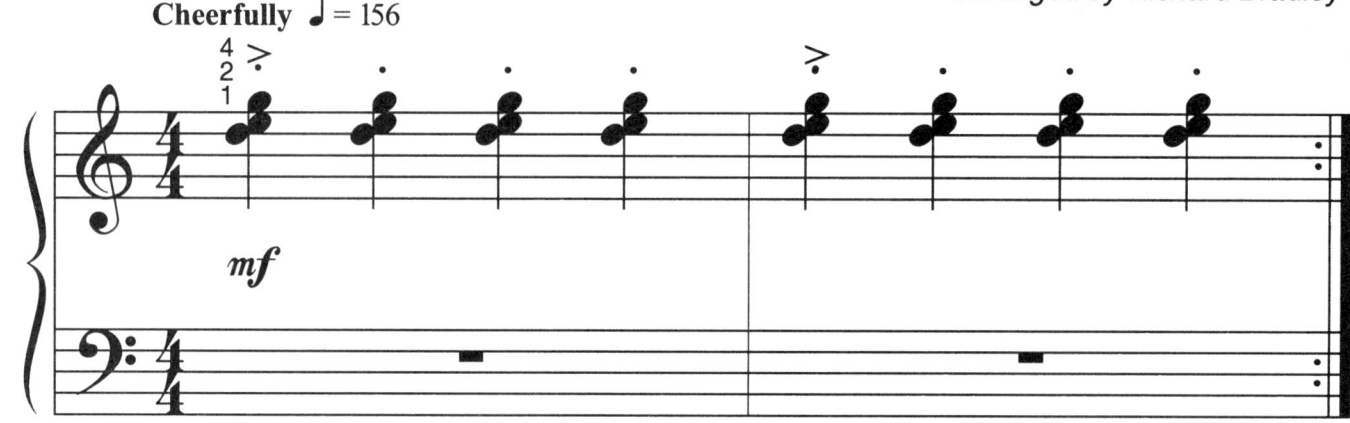

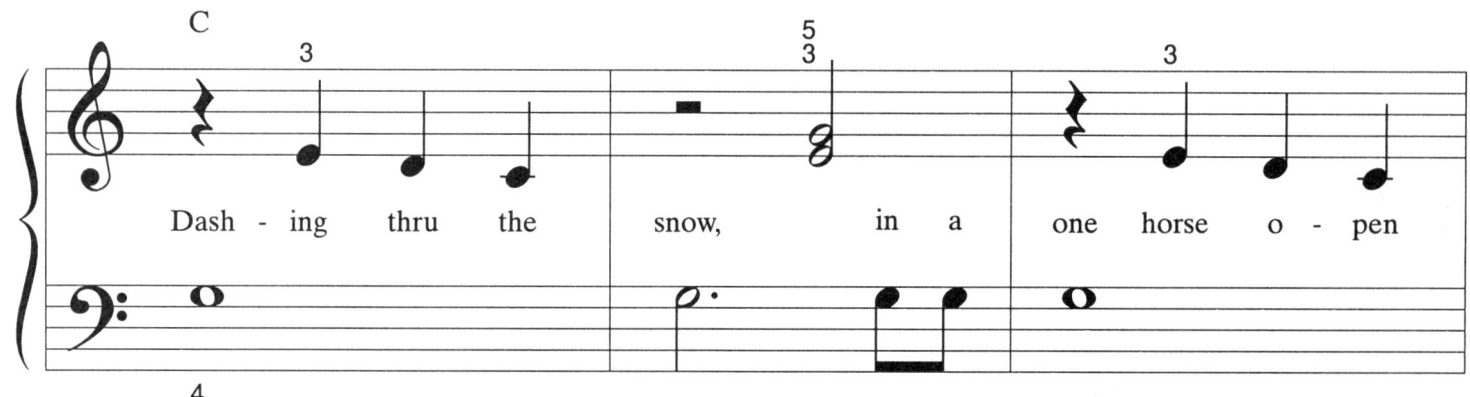

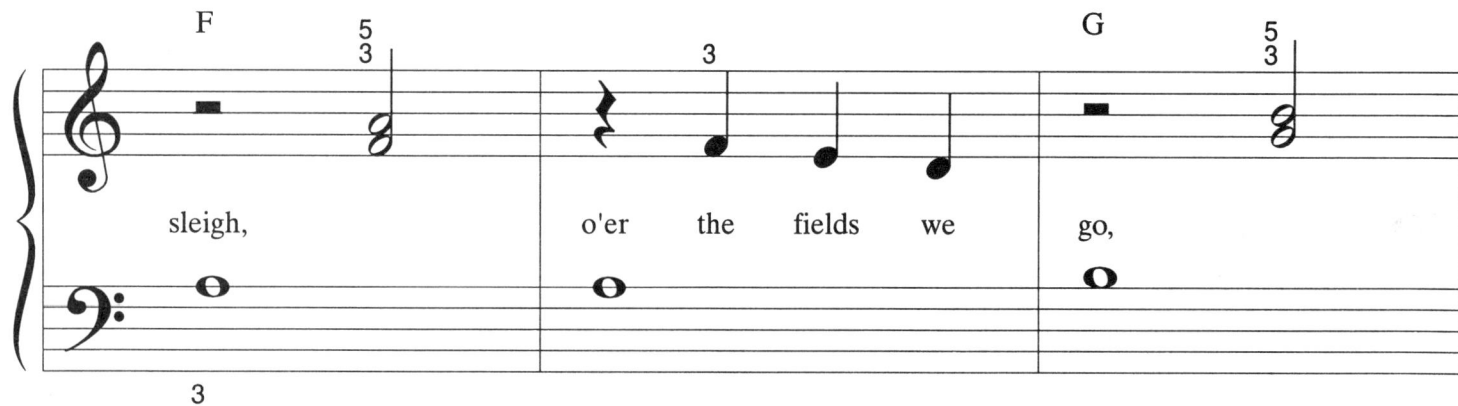

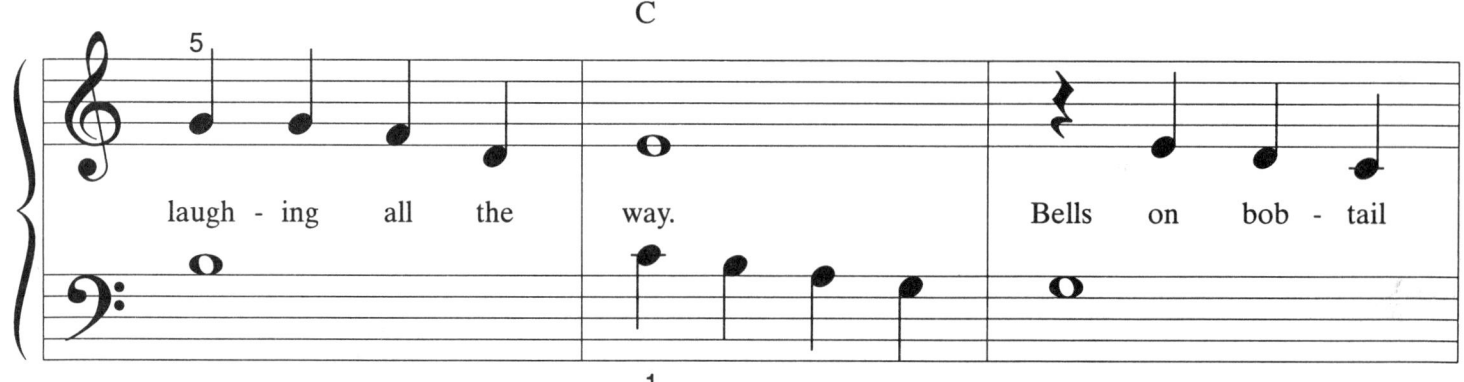

Jingle Bells - 3 - 1

© 2003 BRADLEY PUBLICATIONS
All Rights Assigned to and Controlled by BEAM ME UP MUSIC (ASCAP),
c/o WARNER BROS. PUBLICATIONS U.S. INC., 15800 N.W. 48th Avenue, Miami, FL 33014
All Rights Reserved

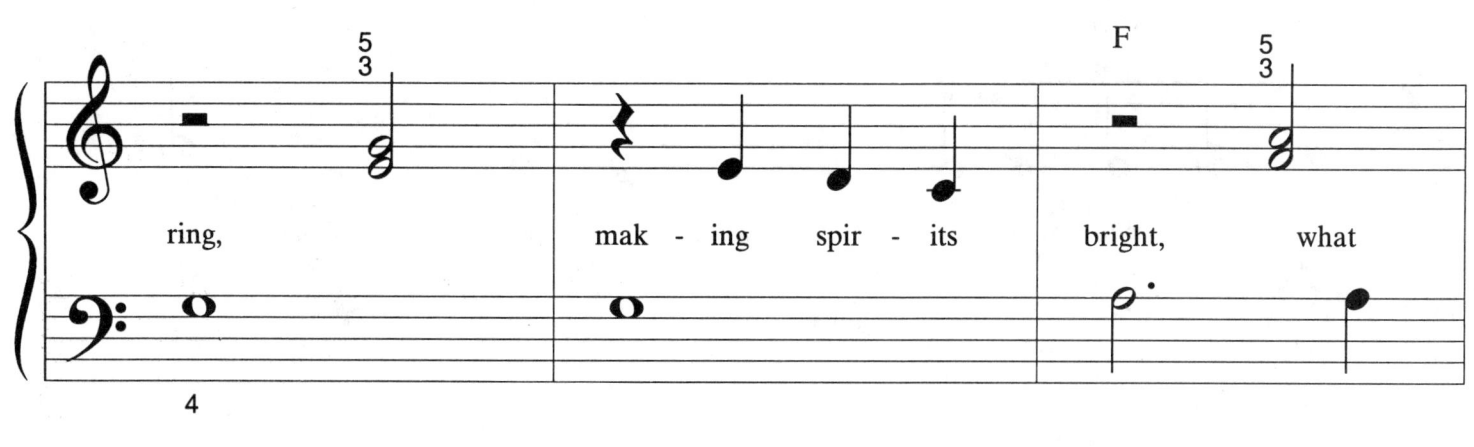

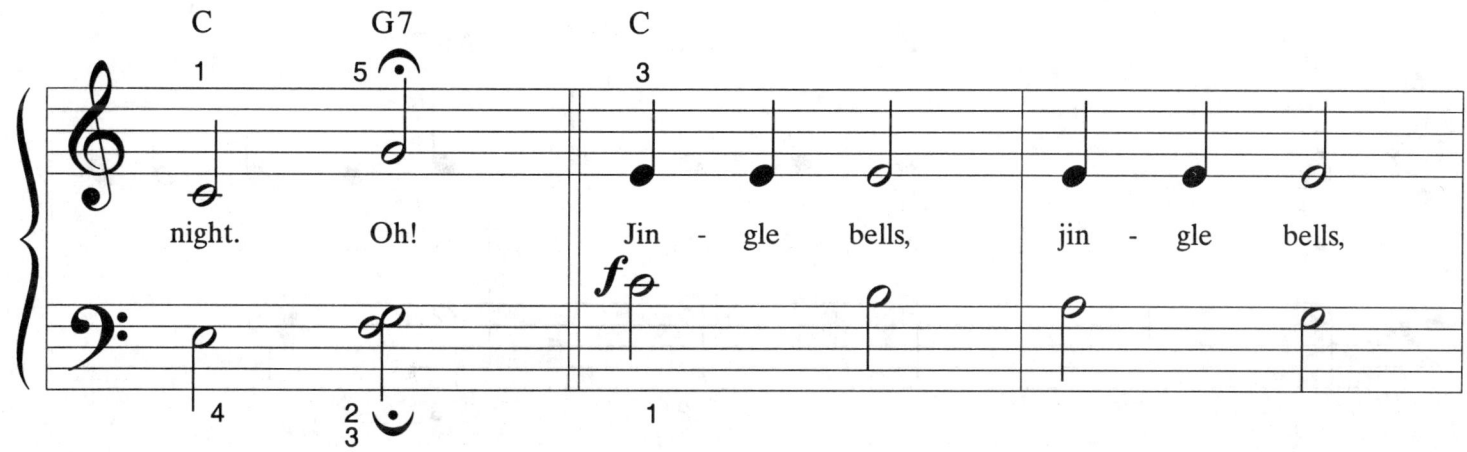
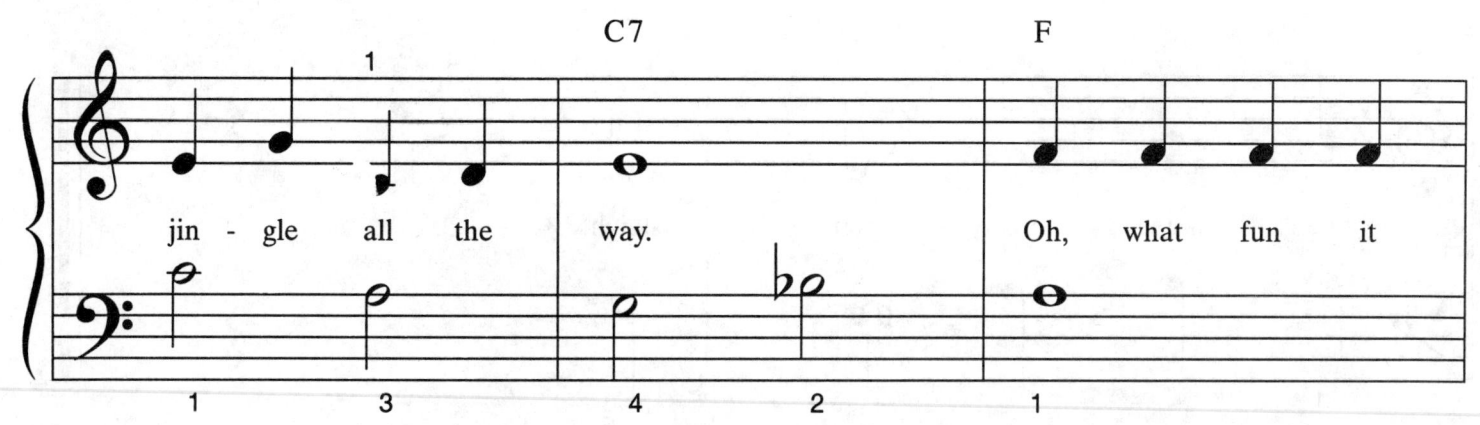

30

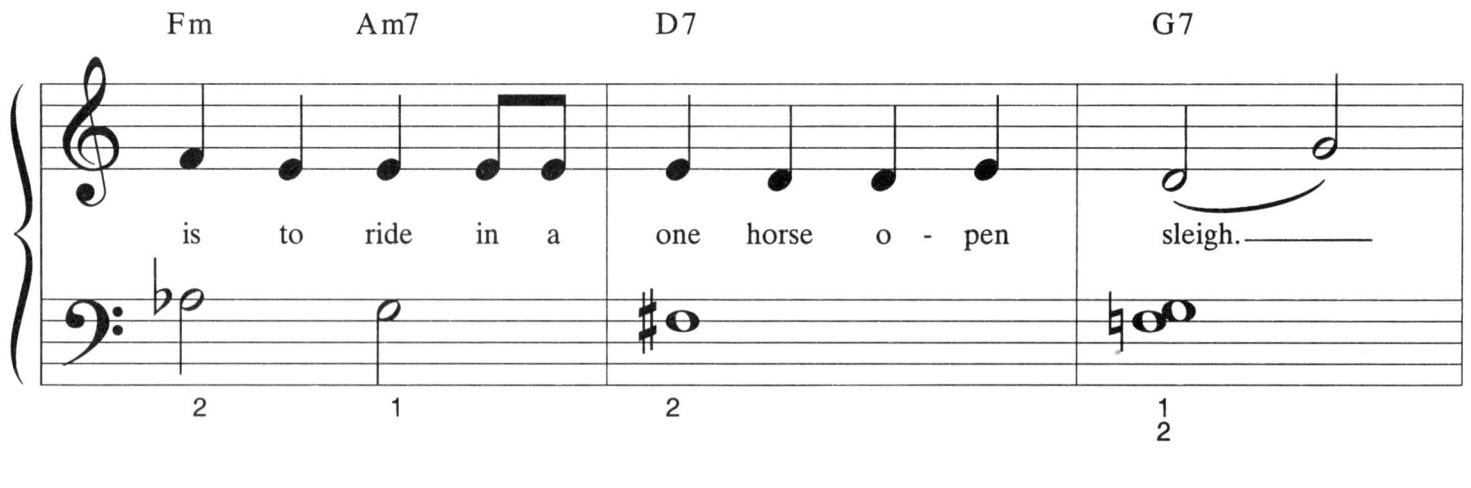
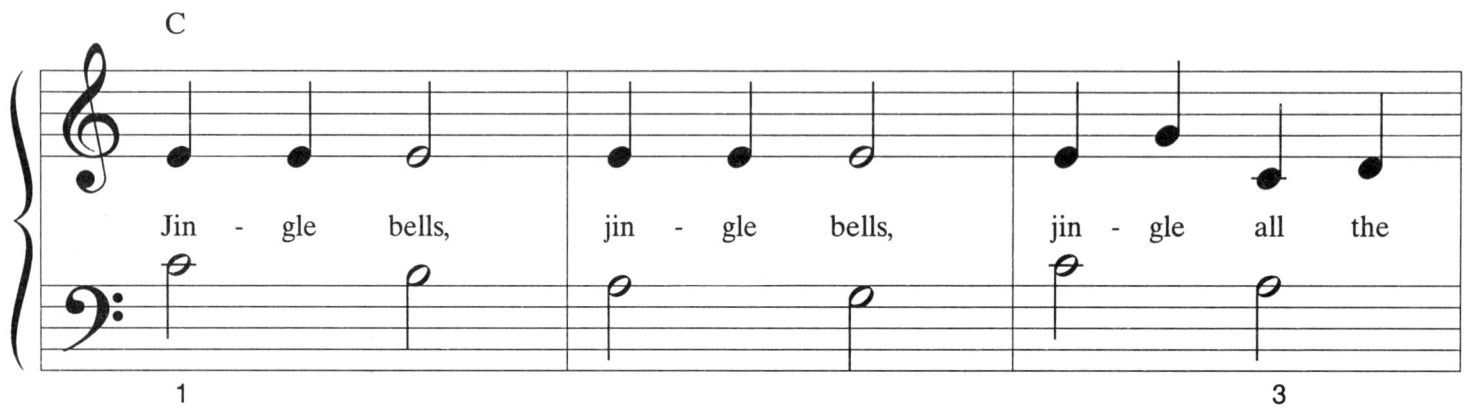

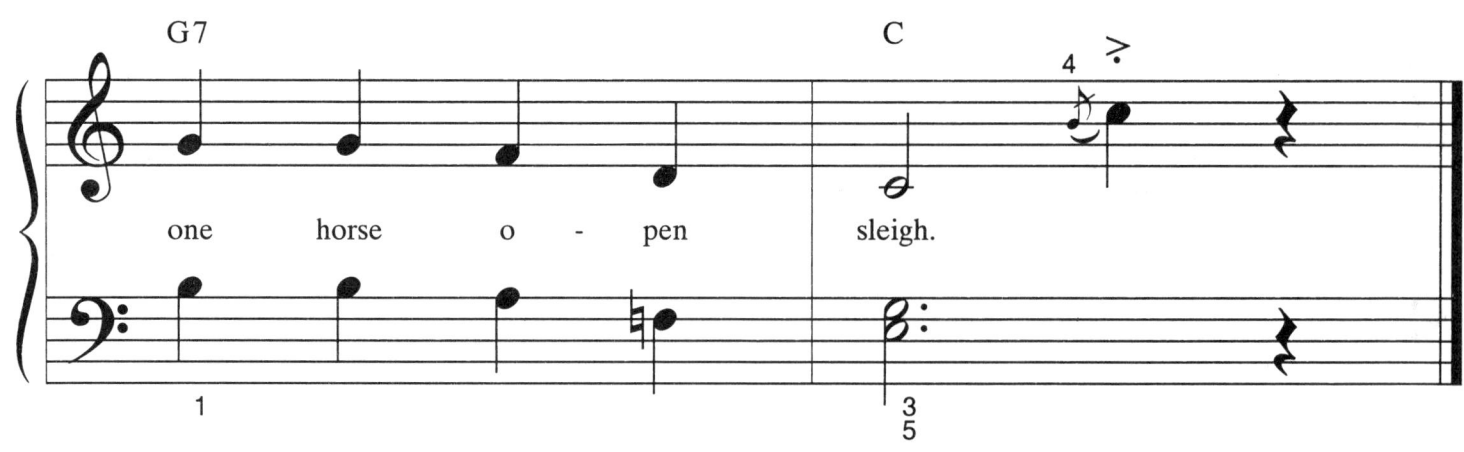

Jingle Bells - 3 - 3

UKRAINIAN BELL CAROL

TRADITIONAL UKRAINIAN CAROL
Arranged by Richard Bradley

32

O CHRISTMAS TREE

TRADITIONAL
Arranged by Richard Bradley

D7
sight of thee at Christ - mas tide spreads
G
hope and glad - ness far and wide. O
D7 G
Christ - mas tree, O Christ - mas tree! Thou
D7 G
tree most fair and love - ly!

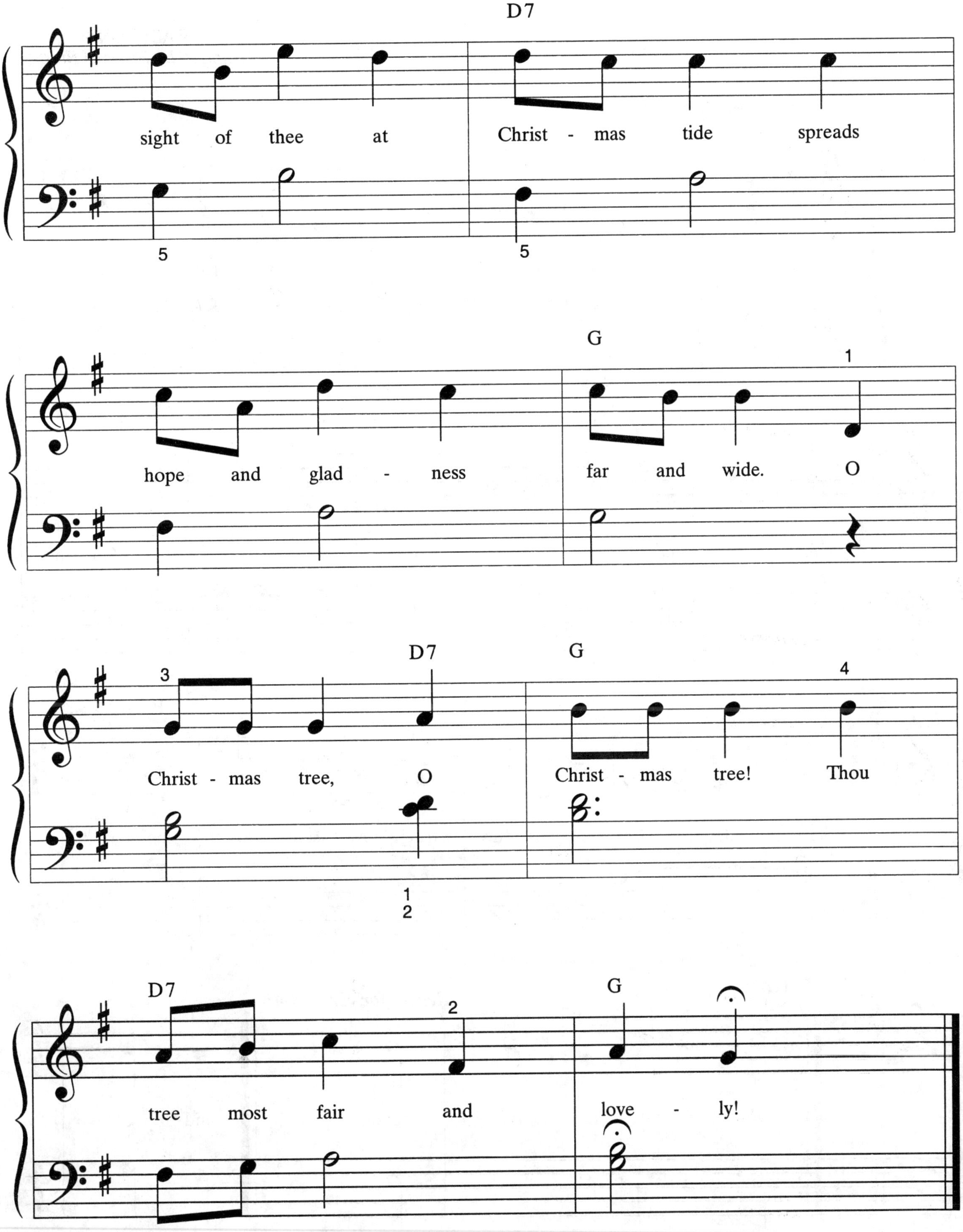

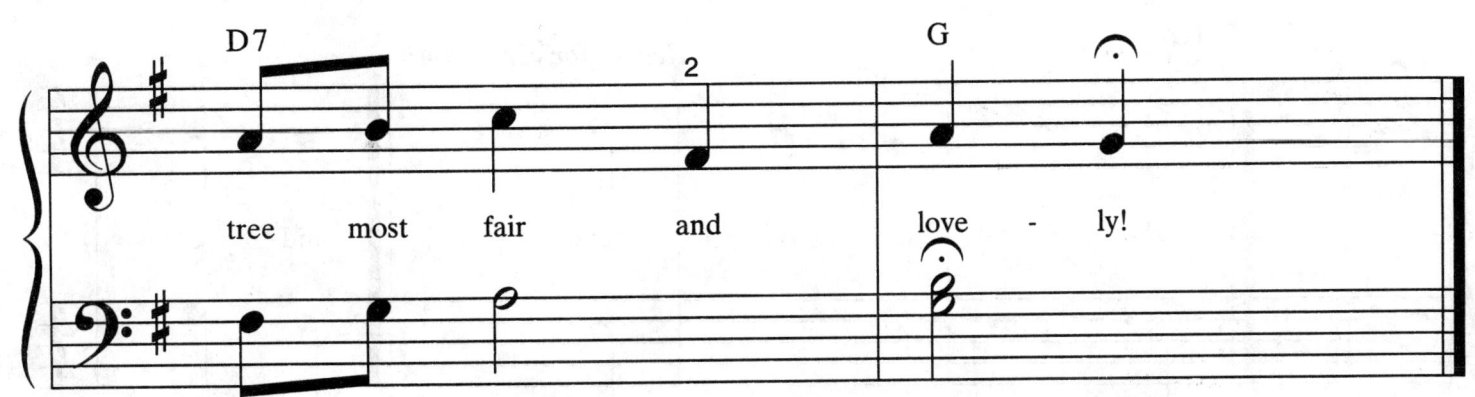

THE TWELVE DAYS OF CHRISTMAS

TRADITIONAL
Arranged by Richard Bradley

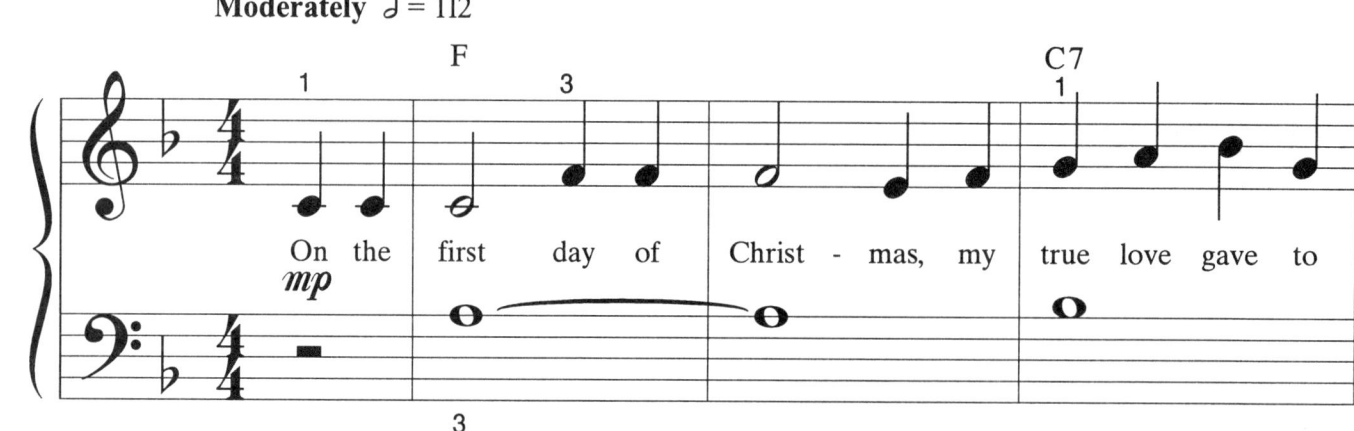
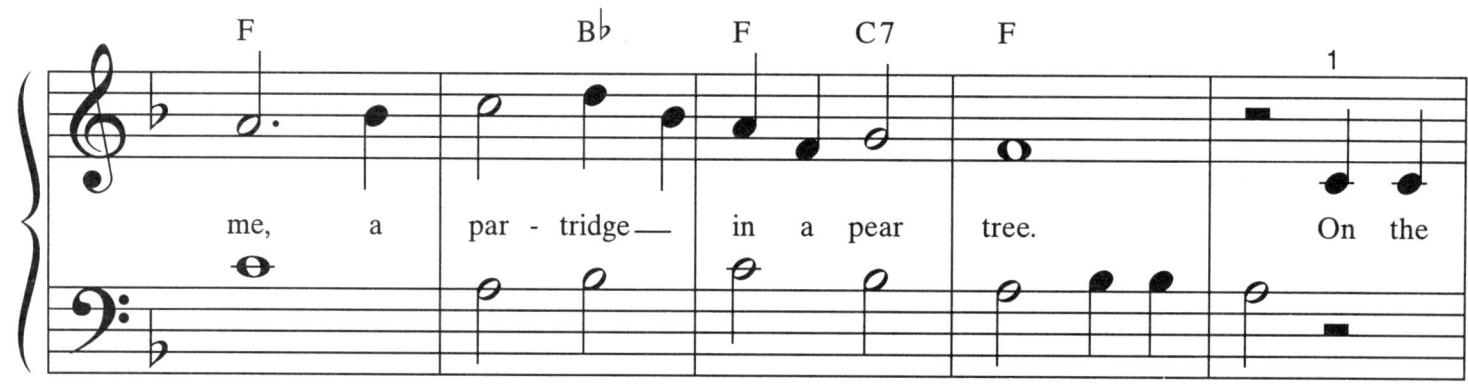
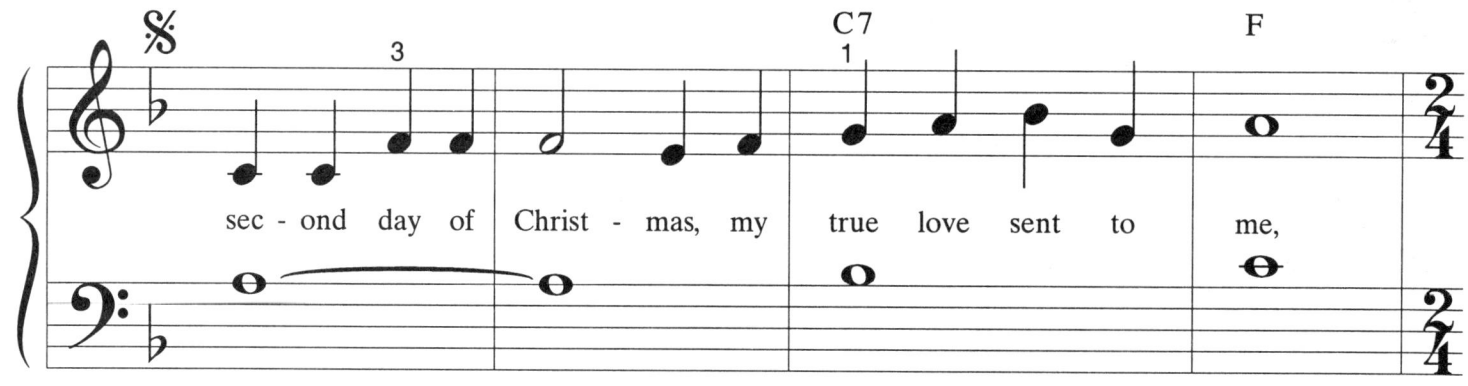
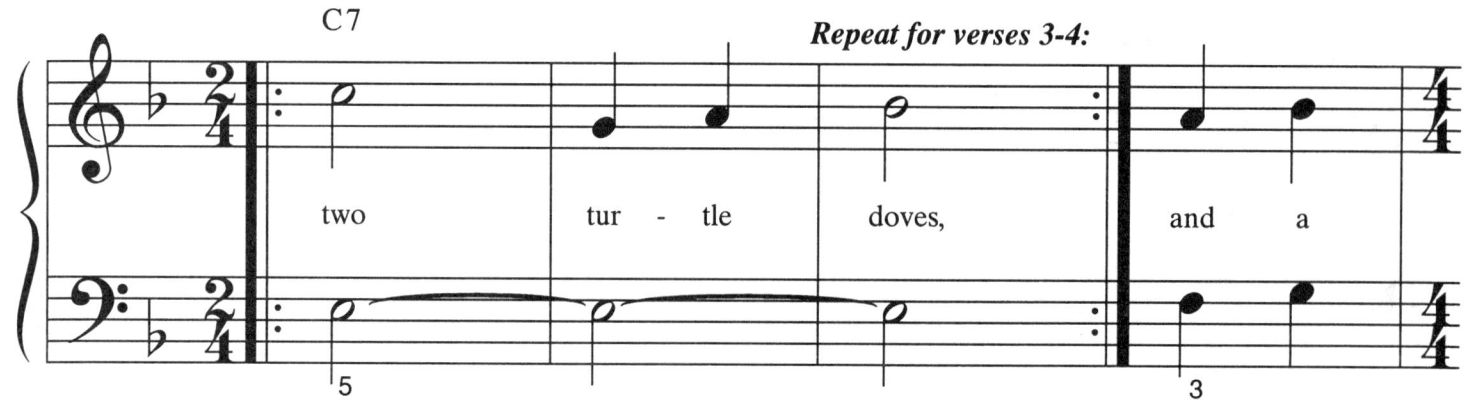

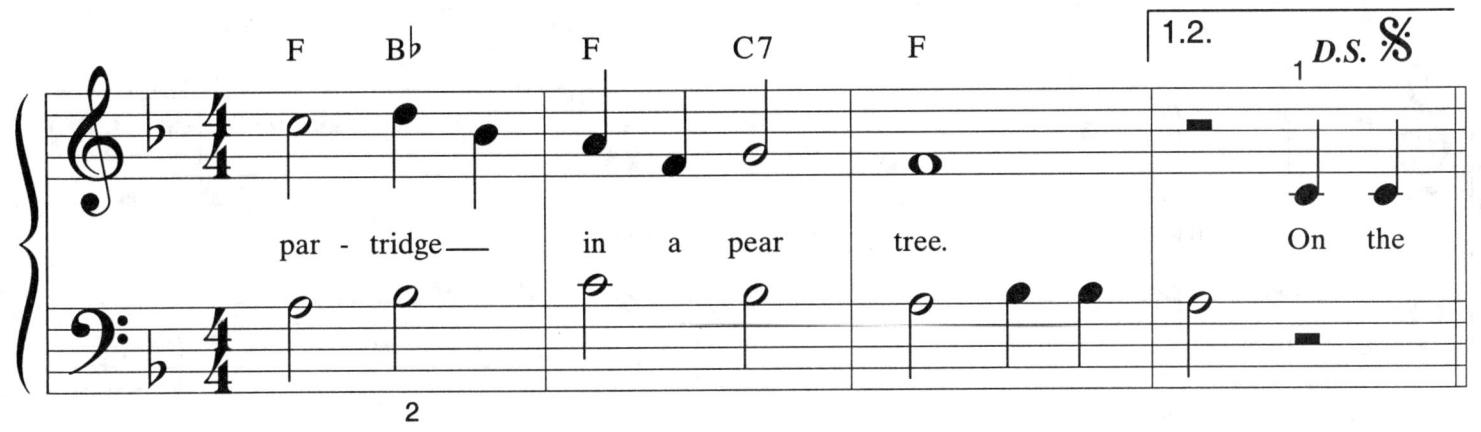

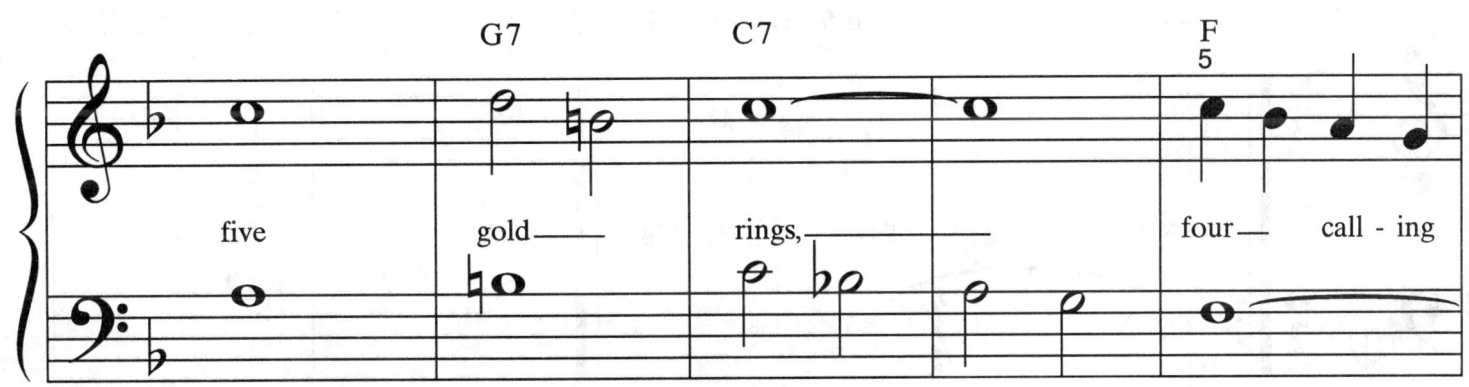
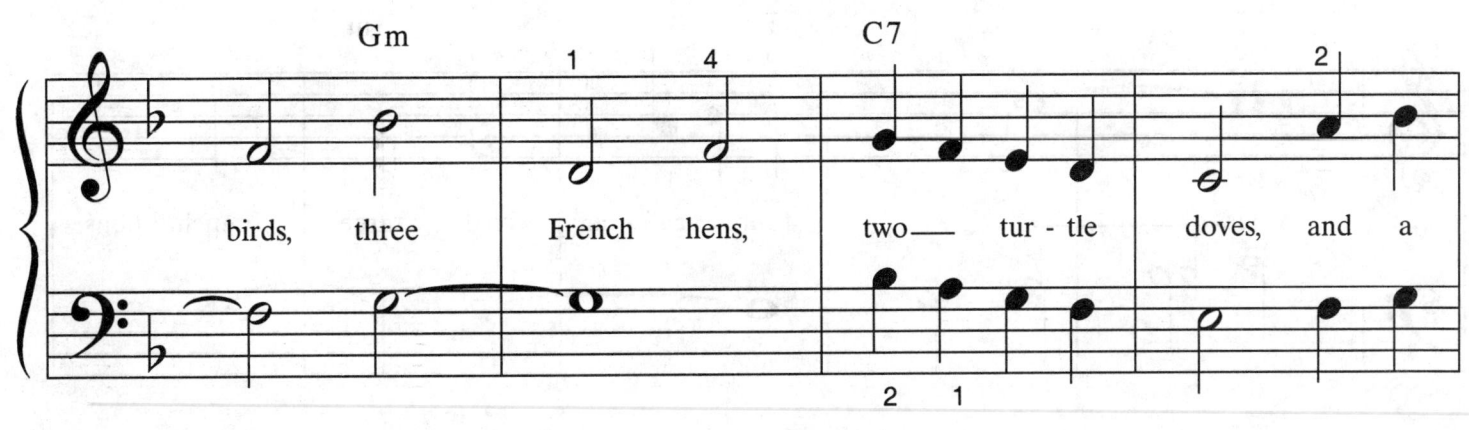

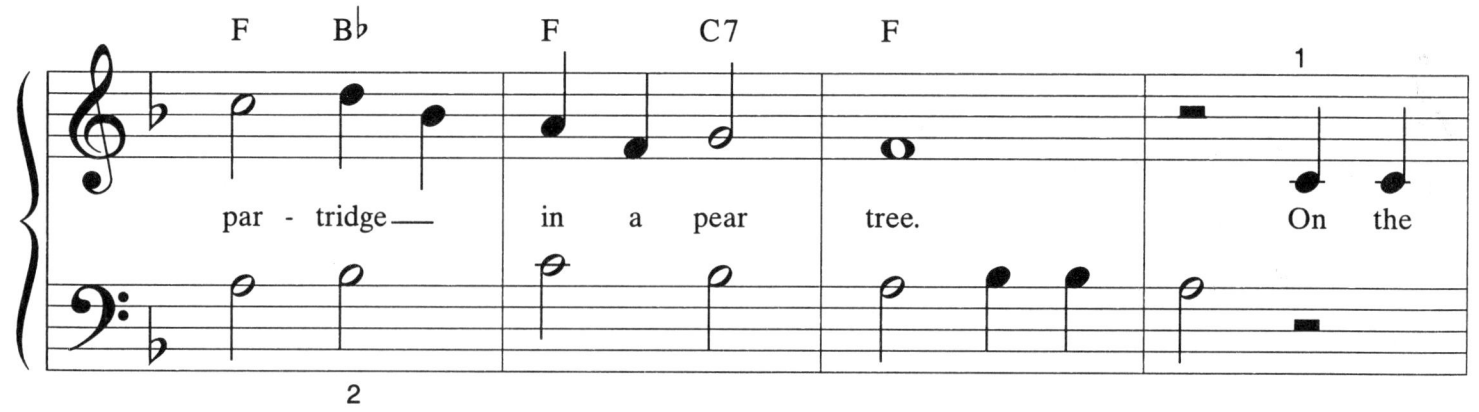

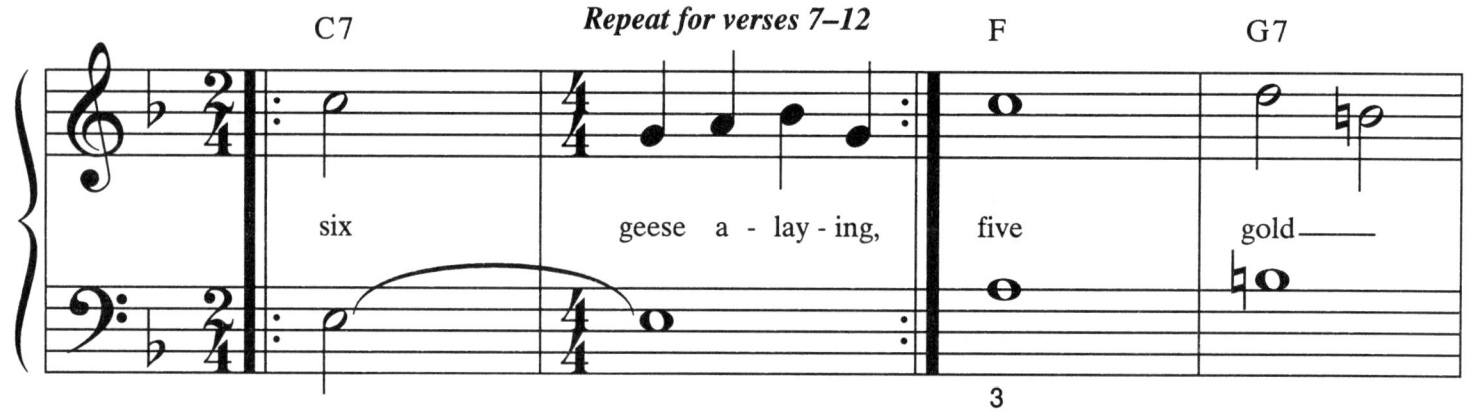
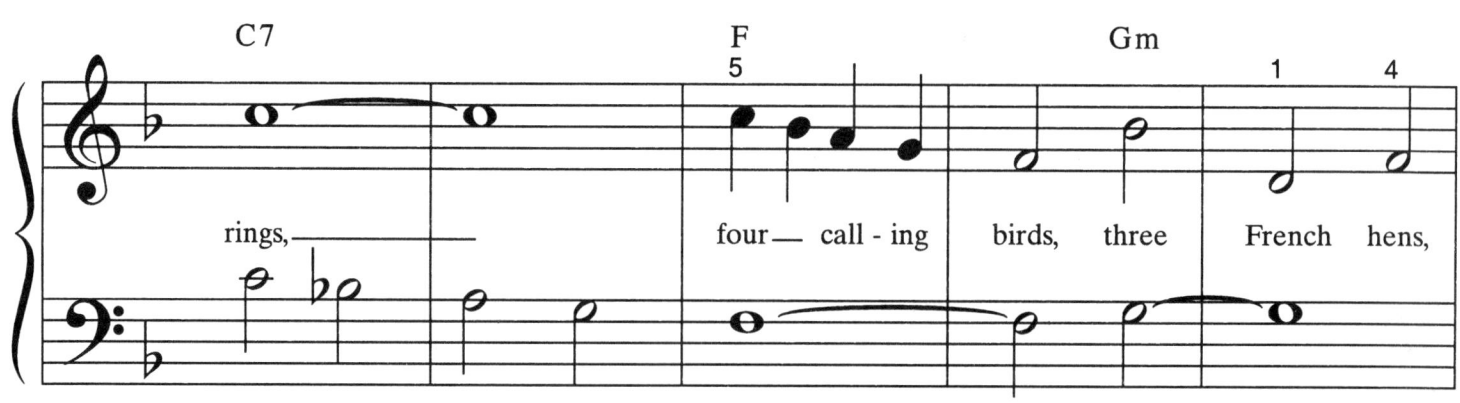

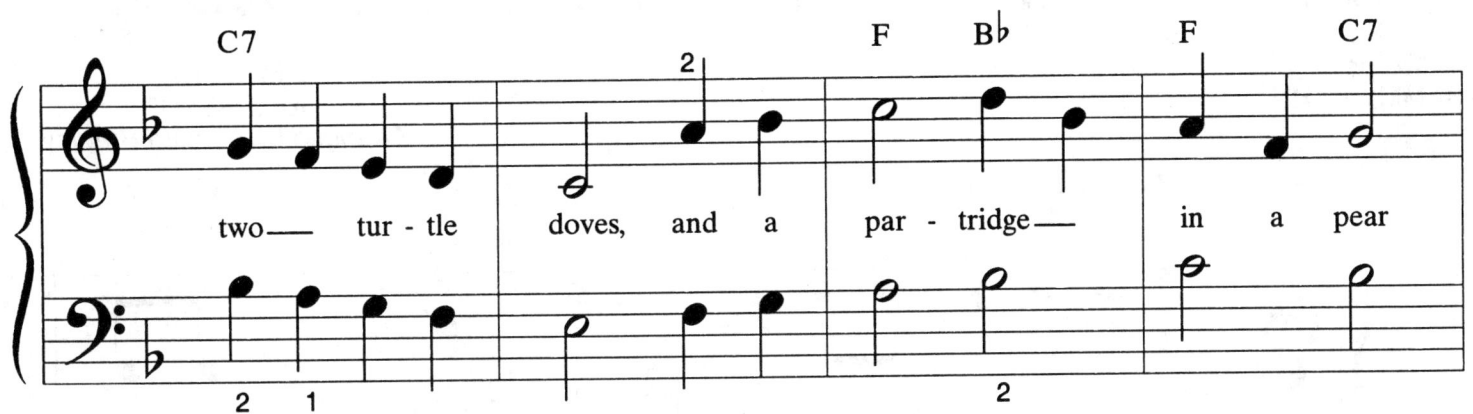

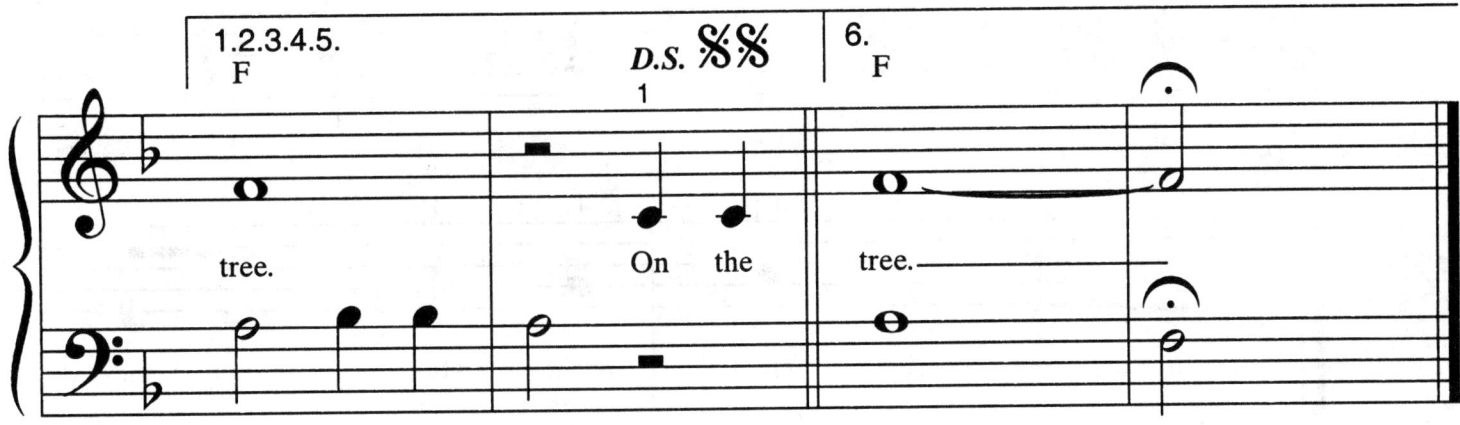

3. Third day of Christmas, my true love sent to me, three French hens,

4. Fourth day of Christmas, my true love sent to me, four calling birds,

7. Seventh day of Christmas, my true love sent to me, seven swans a-swimming,

8. Eighth day of Christmas, my true love sent to me, eight maids a-milking,

9. Ninth day of Christmas, my true love sent to me, nine ladies dancing,

10. Tenth day of Christmas, my true love sent to me, ten lords a-leaping,

11. Eleventh day of Christmas, my true love sent to me, eleven pipers piping,

12. Twelfth day of Christmas, my true love sent to me, twelve drummers drumming,

LET IT SNOW! LET IT SNOW! LET IT SNOW!

Words by
SAMMY CAHN

Music by
JULE STYNE
Arranged by Richard Bradley

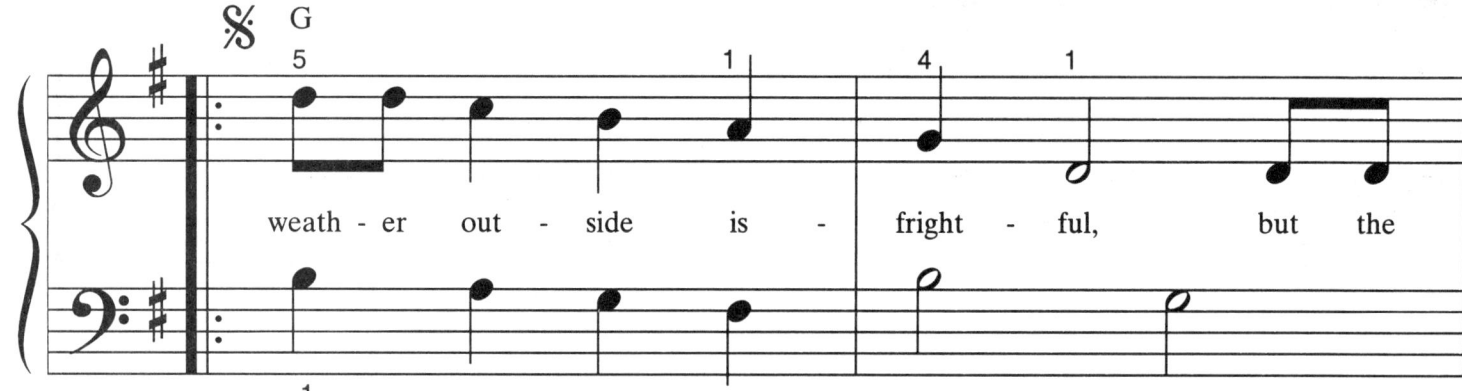

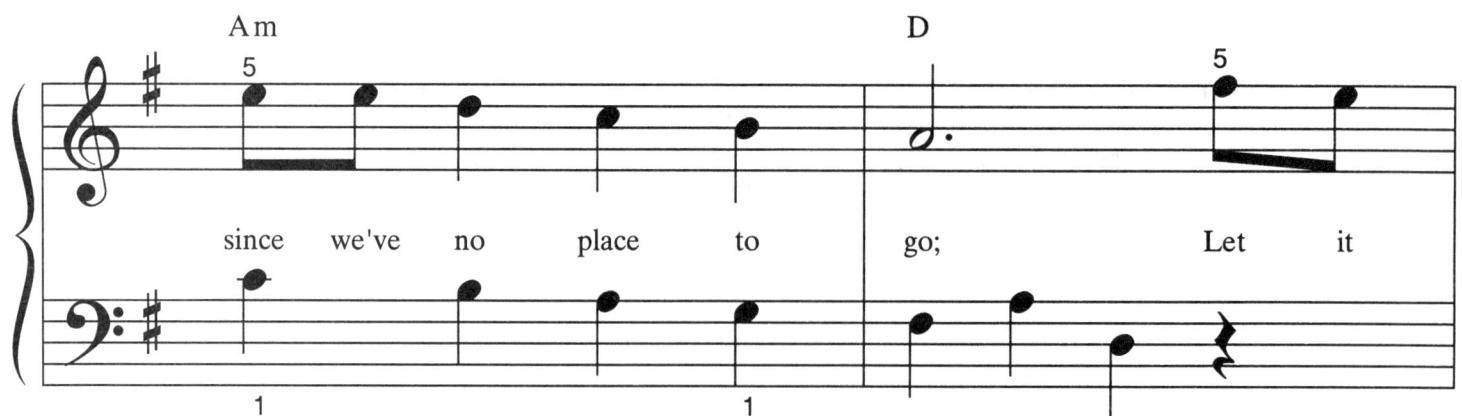

© 1945 CAHN MUSIC COMPANY
Copyright Renewed, assigned to CAHN MUSIC COMPANY & JULE STYNE
This arrangement © 1997 CAHN MUSIC COMPANY & JULE STYNE
All Rights on behalf of CAHN MUSIC COMPANY Administered by CHERRY LANE MUSIC PUBLISHING COMPANY.
JULE STYNE'S interest controlled in the U.S.A. by PRODUCERS MUSIC PUB. CO., INC. and Administered by CHAPPELL & CO., INC.
All Rights Reserved

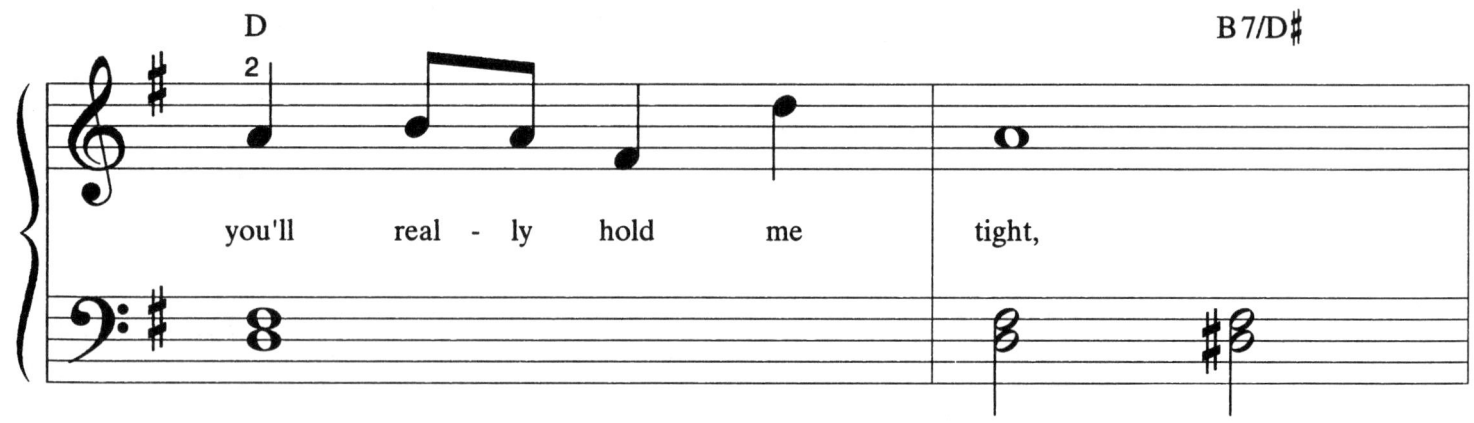

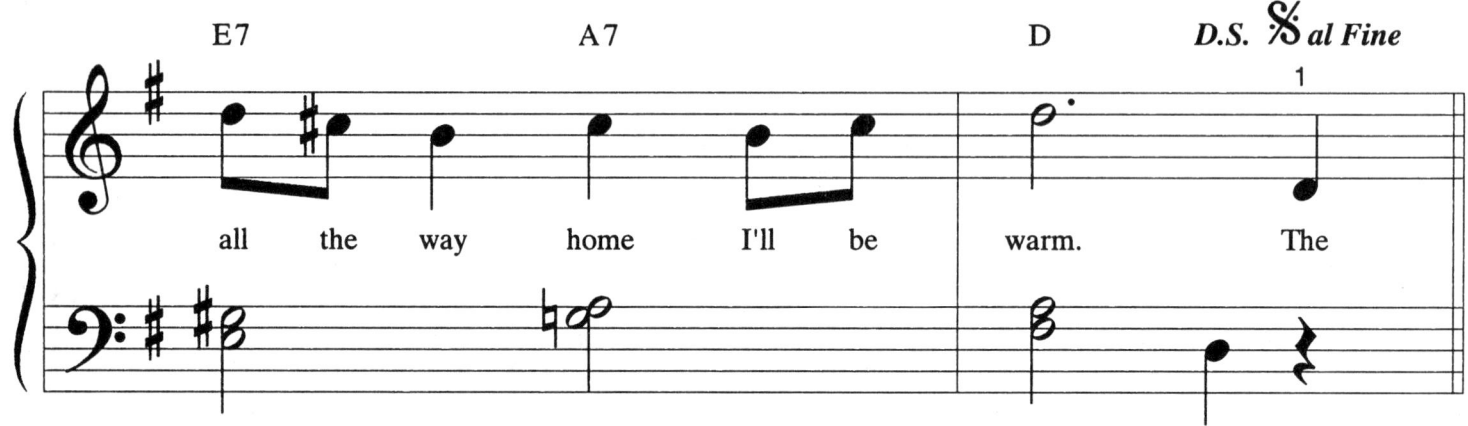

Verse 2:
It doesn't show signs of stopping
And I brought some corn for popping;
The lights are turned way down low,
Let it snow! Let it snow! Let it snow!

Verse 3:
The fire is slowly dying,
And my dear, we're still goodbyeing.
But as long as you love me so,
Let it snow! Let it snow! Let it snow!

SUZY SNOWFLAKE

Words and Music by
SID TEPPER and ROY BRODSKY
Arranged by Richard Bradley

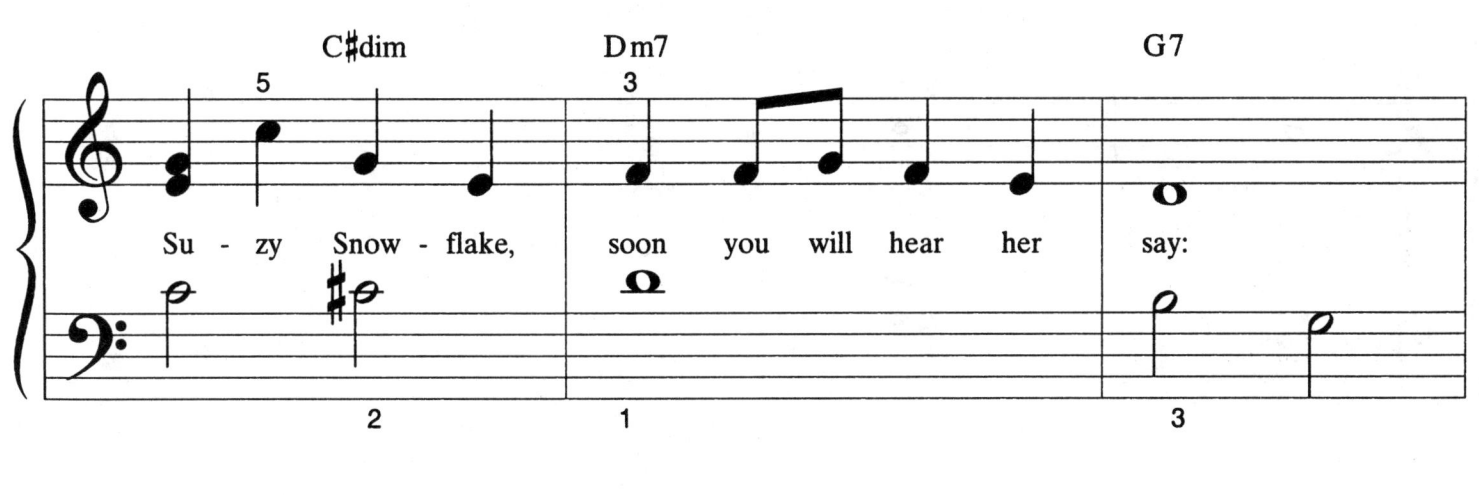
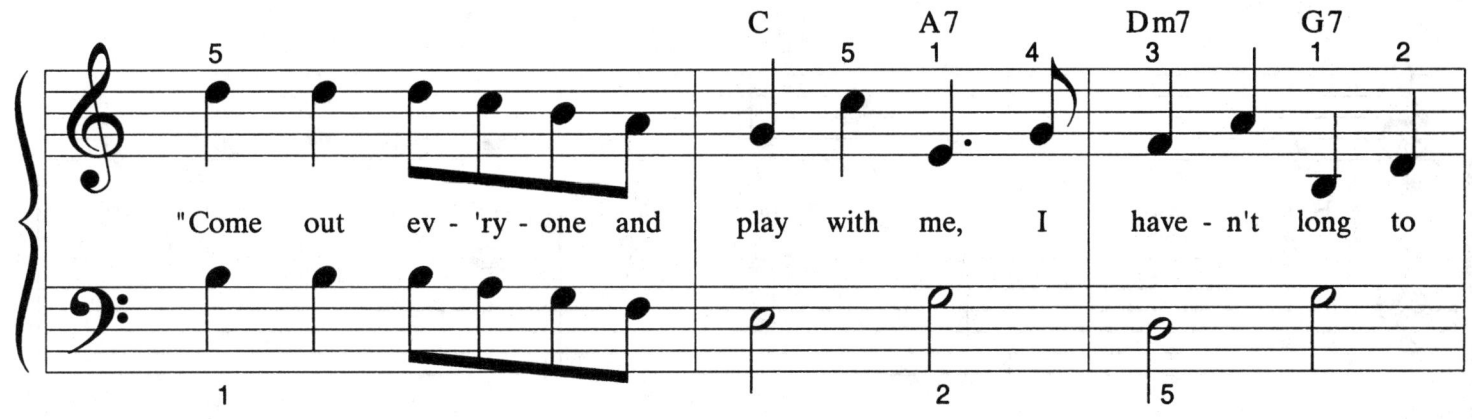
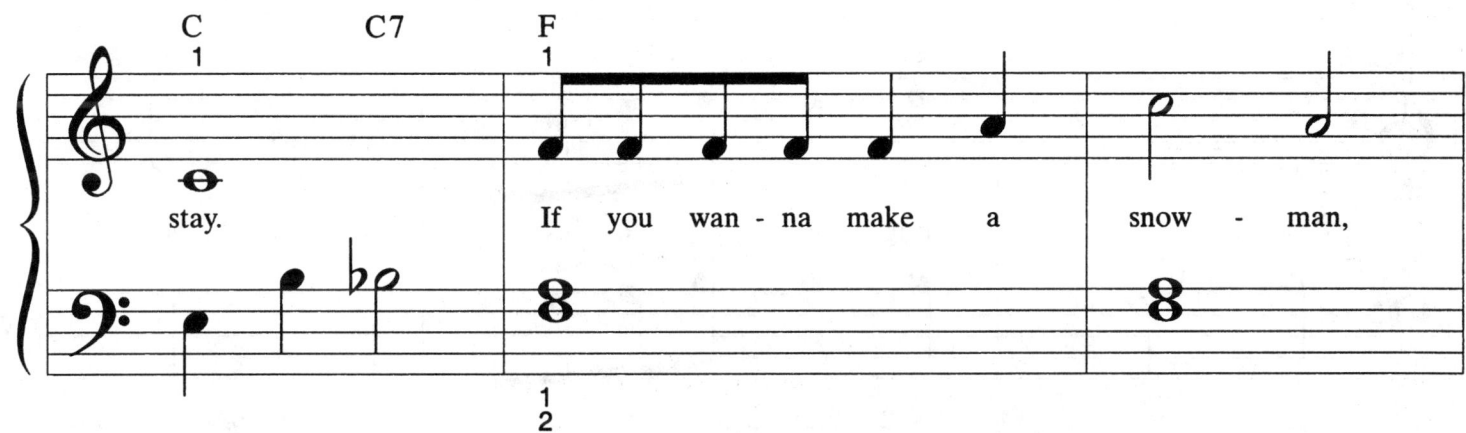

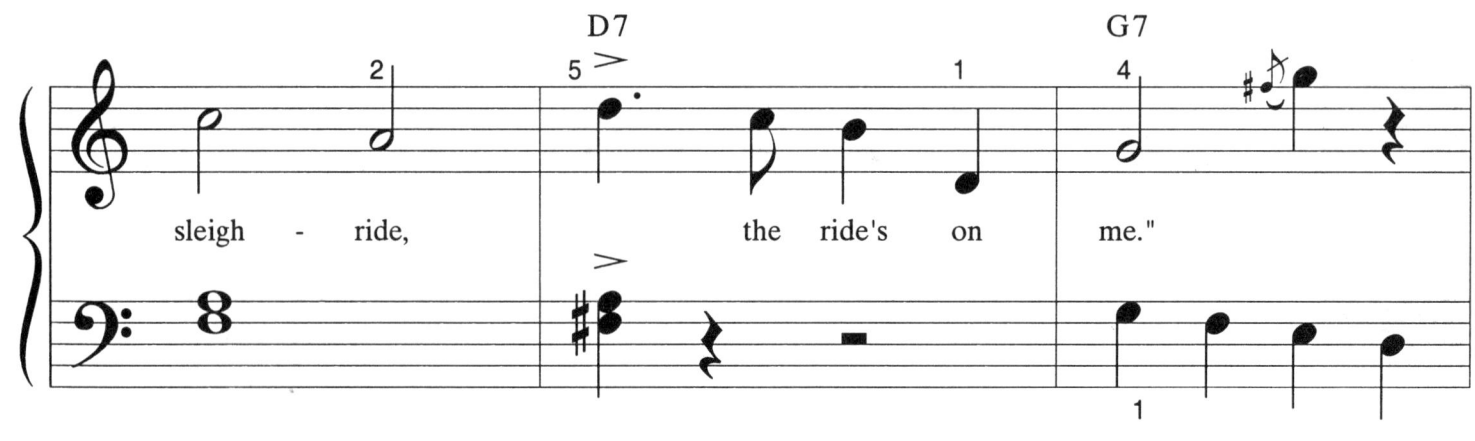

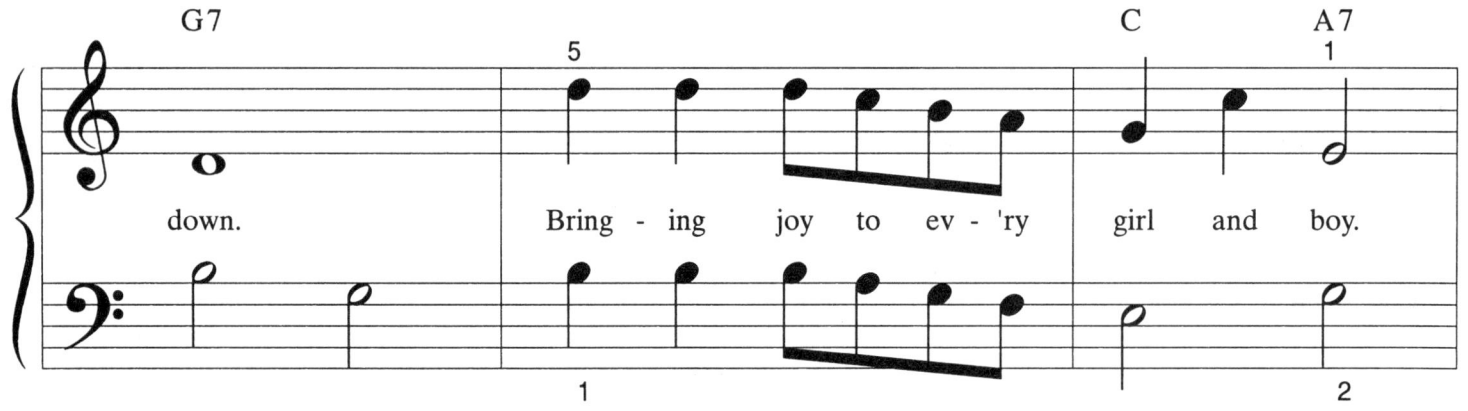
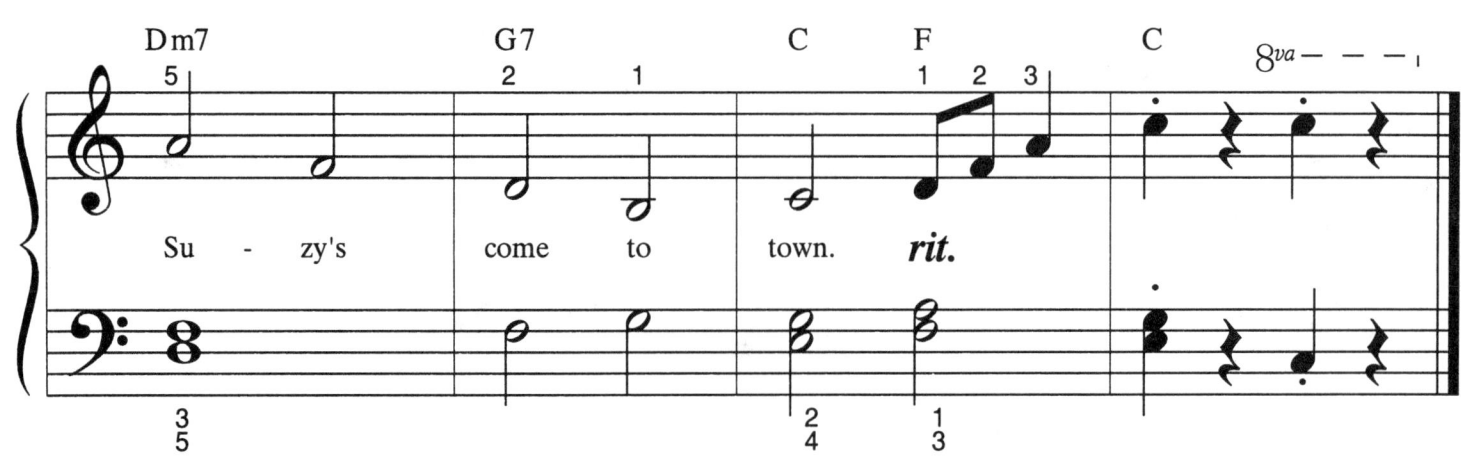

GO TELL IT ON THE MOUNTAIN

TRADITIONAL SPIRITUAL
Arranged by Richard Bradley

Go Tell It on the Mountain - 3 - 1

© 1998 BRADLEY PUBLICATIONS
All Rights Assigned to and Controlled by BEAM ME UP MUSIC (ASCAP),
c/o WARNER BROS. PUBLICATIONS U.S. INC., 15800 N.W. 48th Avenue, Miami, FL 33014
All Rights Reserved

50

Go Tell It on the Mountain - 3 - 3

THE FIRST NOEL

TRADITIONAL
Arranged by Richard Bradley

Santa Claus Is Comin' to Town - 2 - 2

NUTTIN' FOR CHRISTMAS

Words and Music by
SID TEPPER and ROY C. BENNETT
Arranged by Richard Bradley

Nuttin' for Christmas - 4 - 1

© 1955 ROSS JUNGNICKEL, INC.
Copyright Renewed
Copyright and all rights assigned to CHAPPELL & CO. (INTERSONG MUSIC, Publisher)
All Rights Reserved

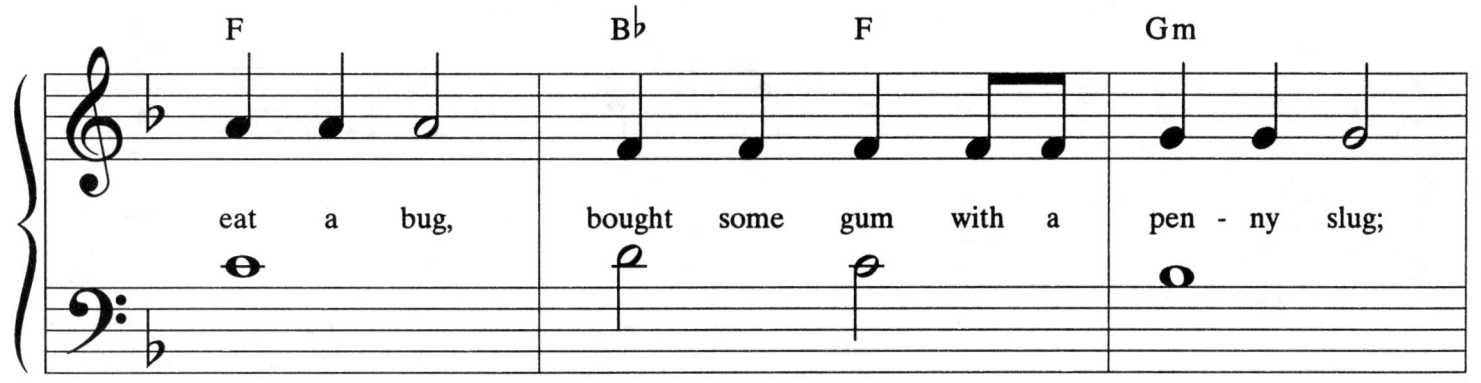
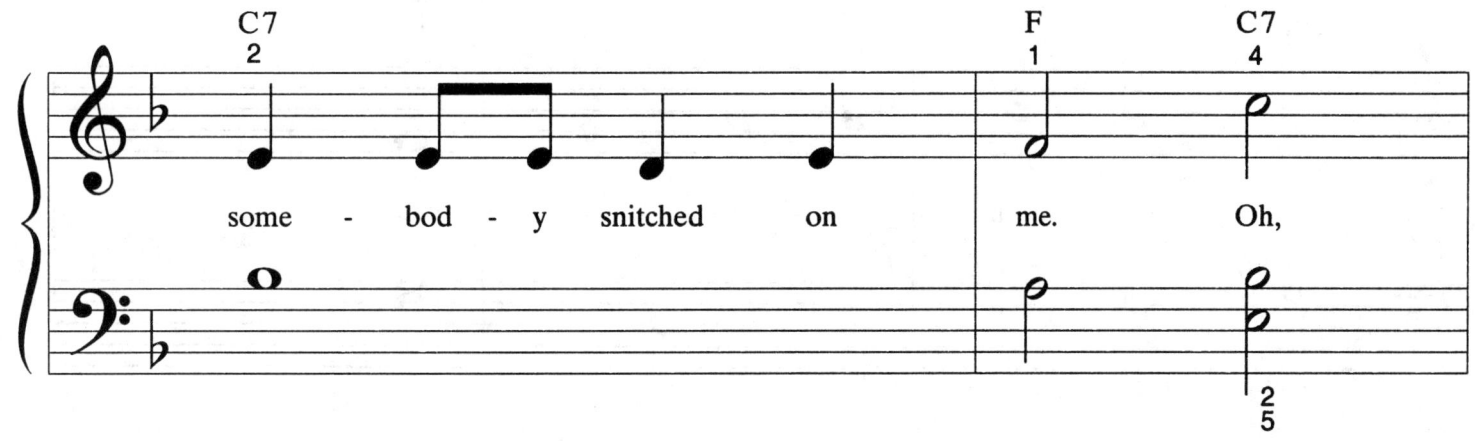
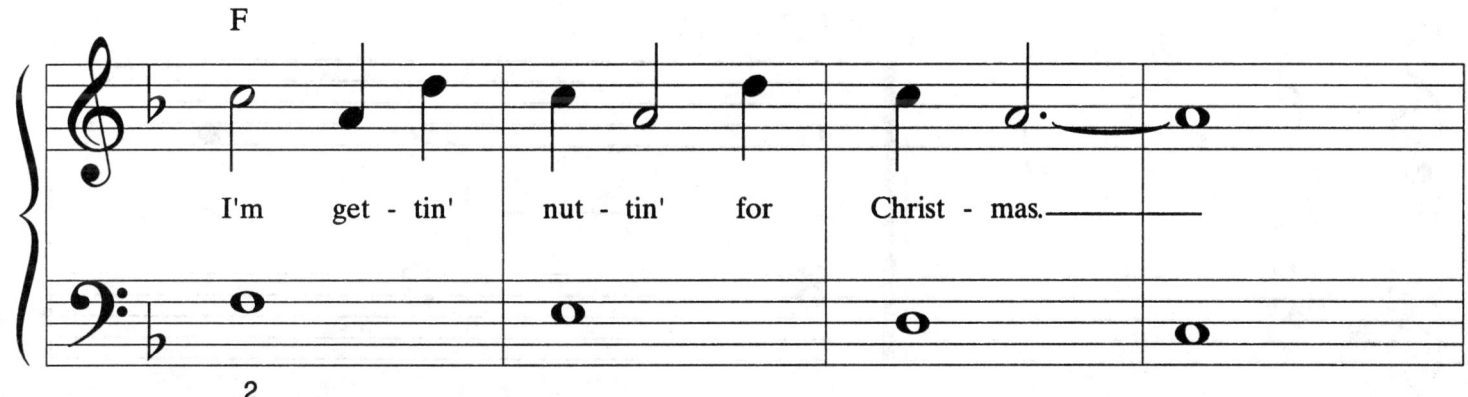
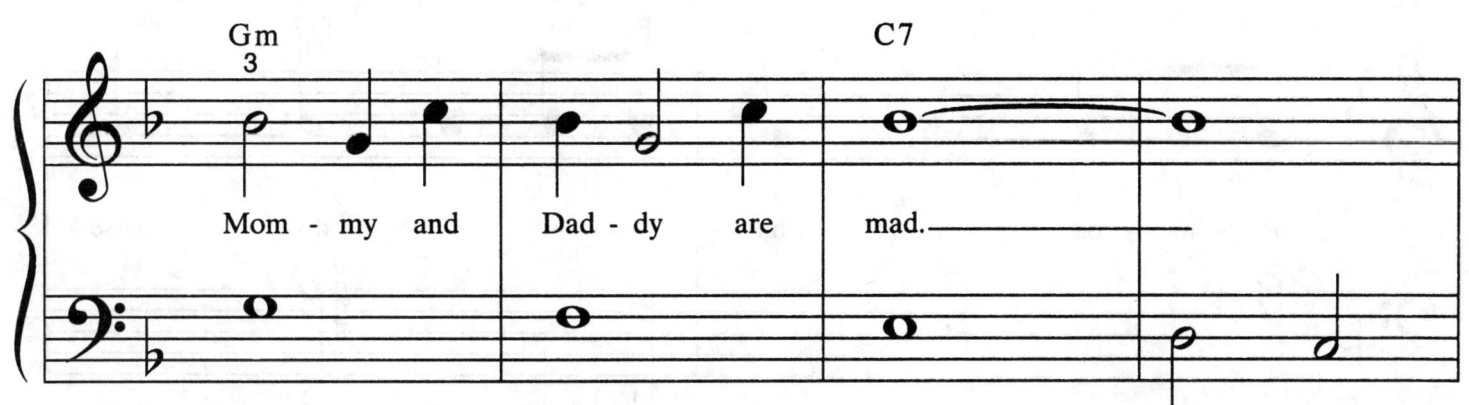

F
I'm get - tin' nut - tin' for Christ - mas, 'cause
3
Gm7
C7
1. 2.
F
I ain't been nut - tin' but bad.
C7
1
3.
F
I
bad. So you
1
3
Gm7
C7
F
D7
bet - ter be good what - ev - er you do, 'cause
1
2
1
3
1
2
1
3

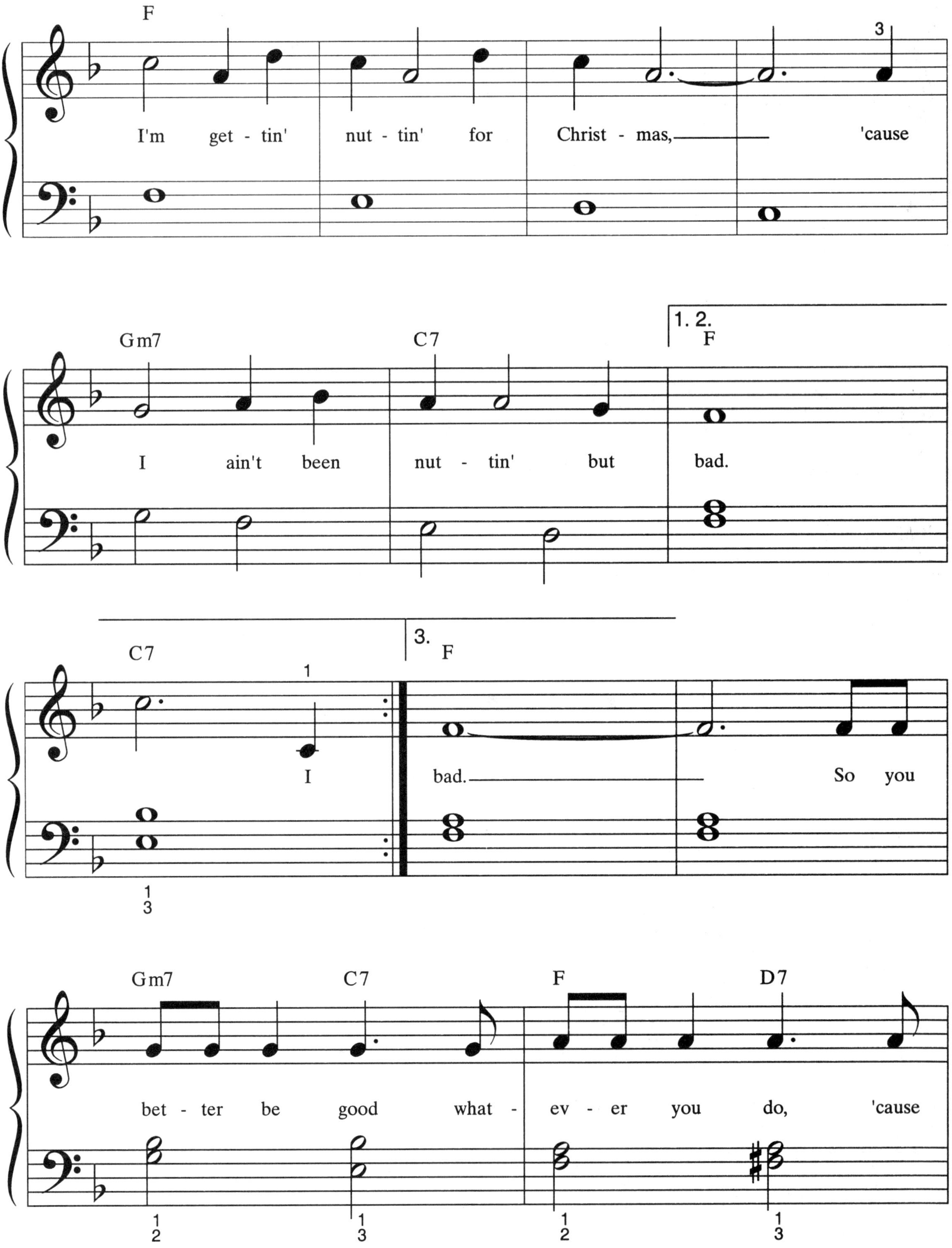

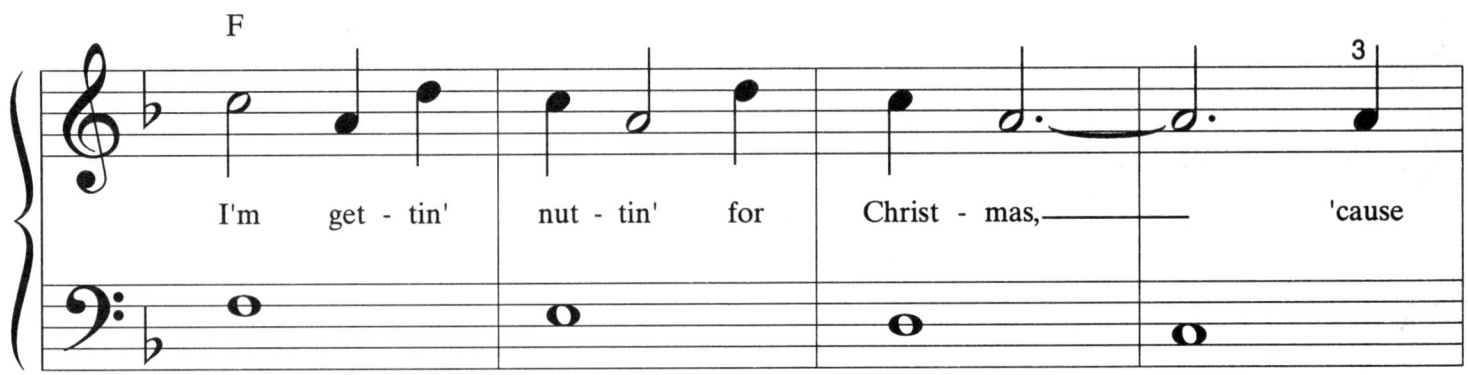

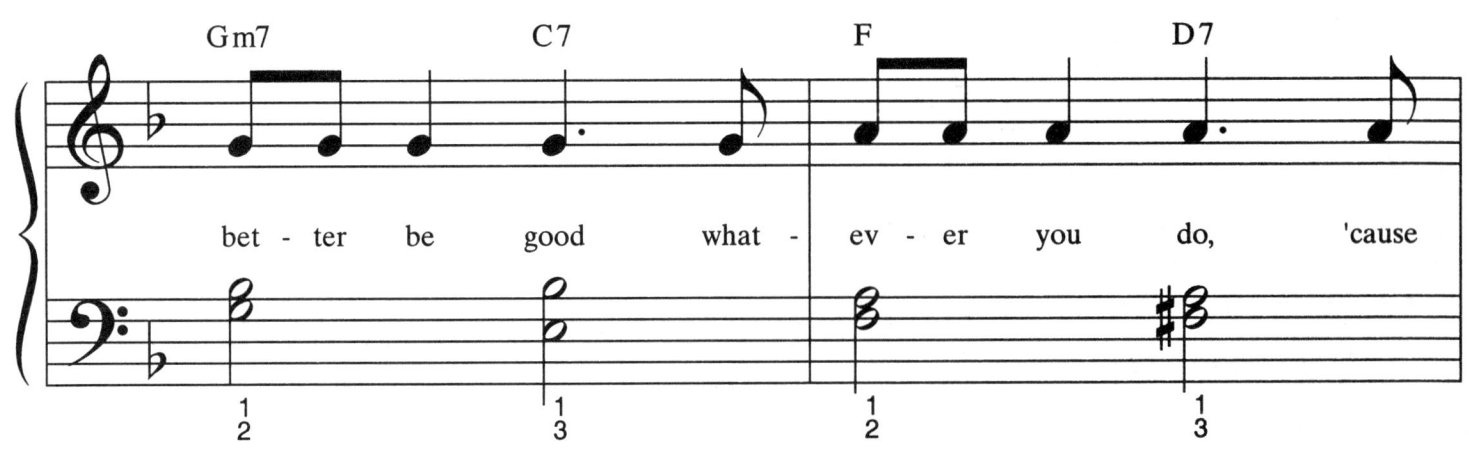

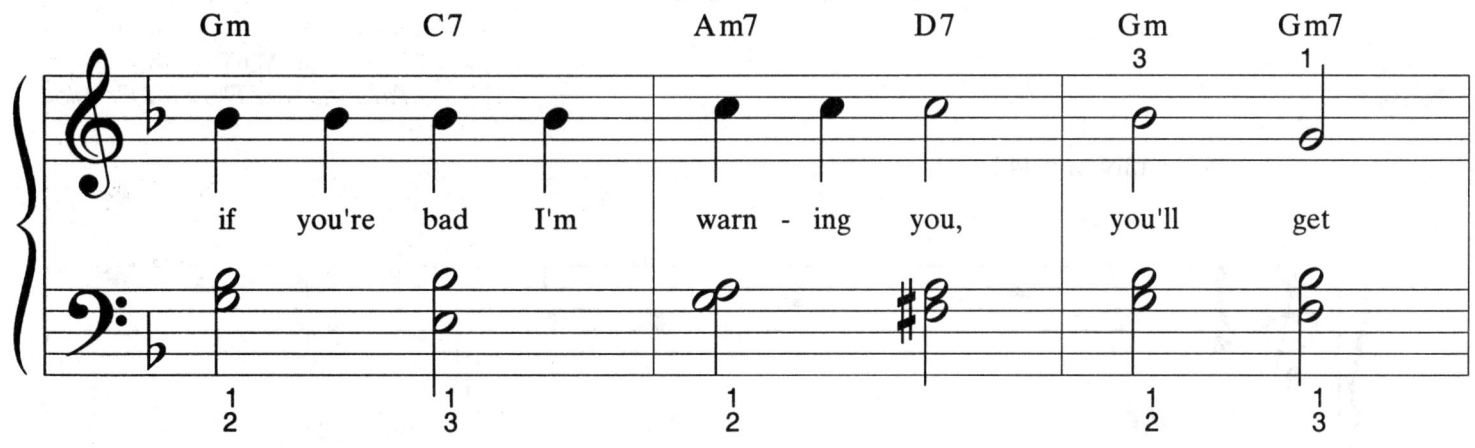

Verse 2:
I put a tack on teacher's chair; somebody snitched on me.
I tied a knot in Susie's hair; somebody snitched on me.
I did a dance on Mommy's plants; climbed a tree and tore my pants.
Filled the sugar bowl with ants; somebody snitched on me. So,...

Verse 3:
I won't be seeing Santa Claus; somebody snitched on me.
He won't come visit me because somebody snitched on me.
Next year I'll be going straight, next year I'll be good, just wait,
I'd start now but it's too late; somebody snitched on me. Oh,...

PAT-A-PAN

TRADITIONAL
Arranged by Richard Bradley

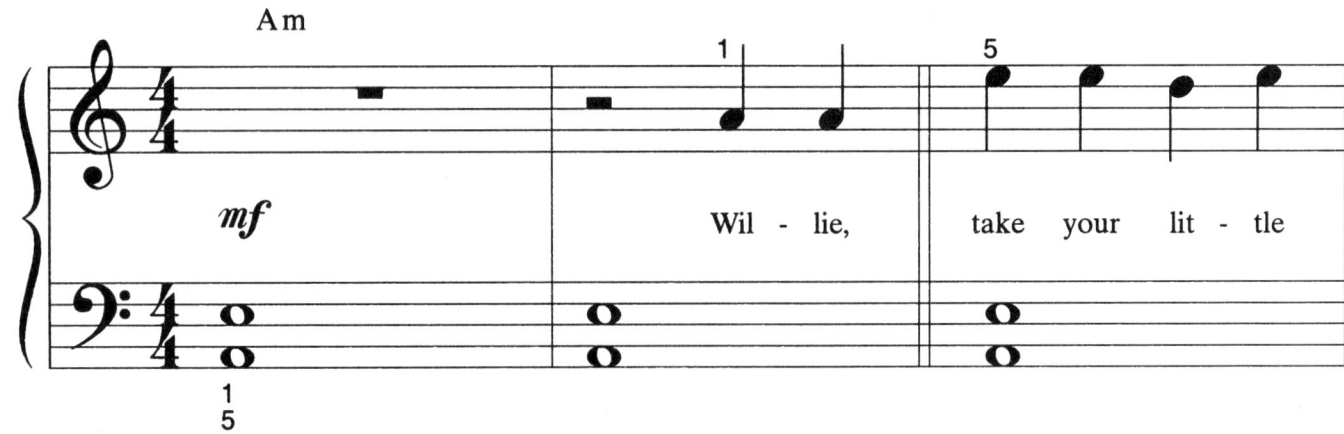
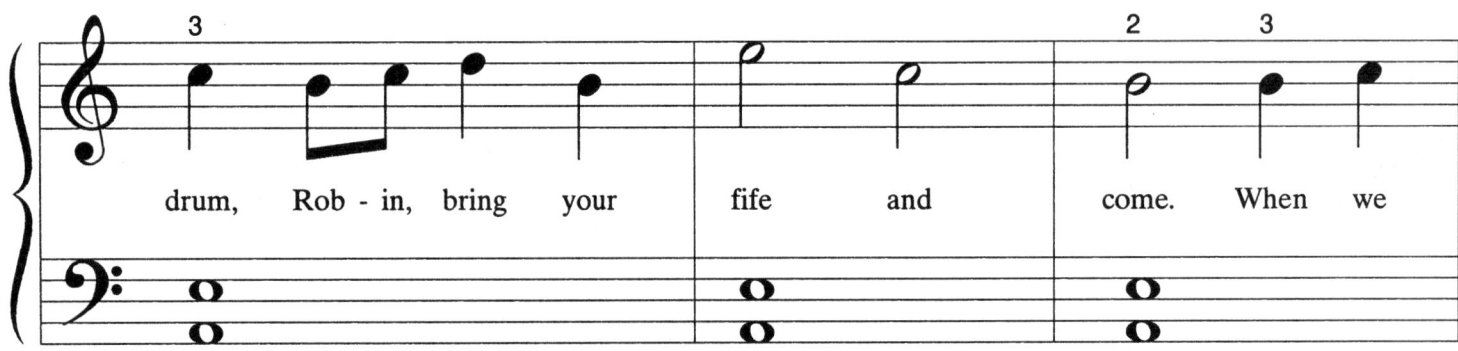

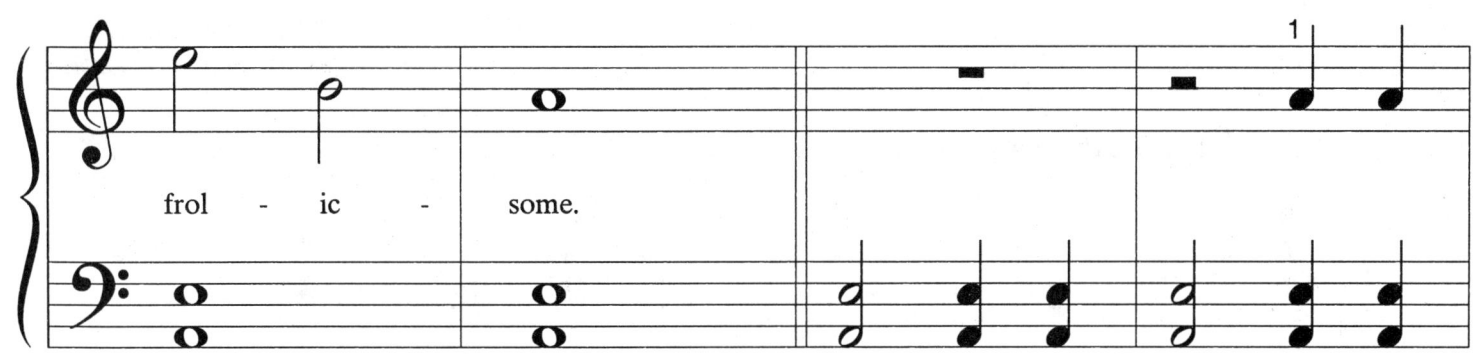

frol - ic - some.

FUM, FUM, FUM

TRADITIONAL
Arranged by Richard Bradley

Fum, Fum, Fum - 2 - 1

© 1998 BRADLEY PUBLICATIONS
All Rights Assigned to and Controlled by BEAM ME UP MUSIC (ASCAP),
c/o WARNER BROS. PUBLICATIONS U.S. INC., 15800 N.W. 48th Avenue, Miami, FL 33014
All Rights Reserved

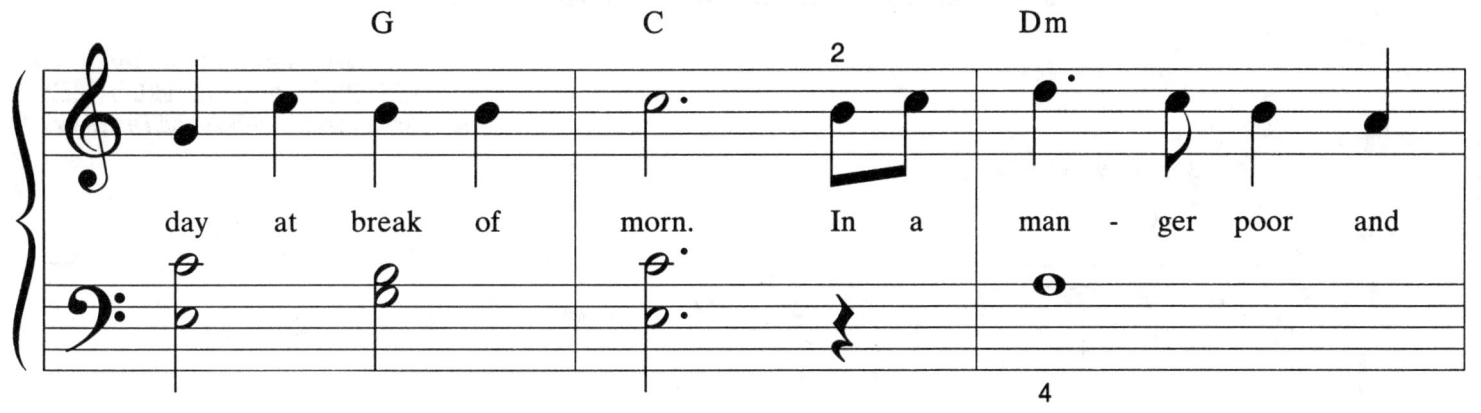
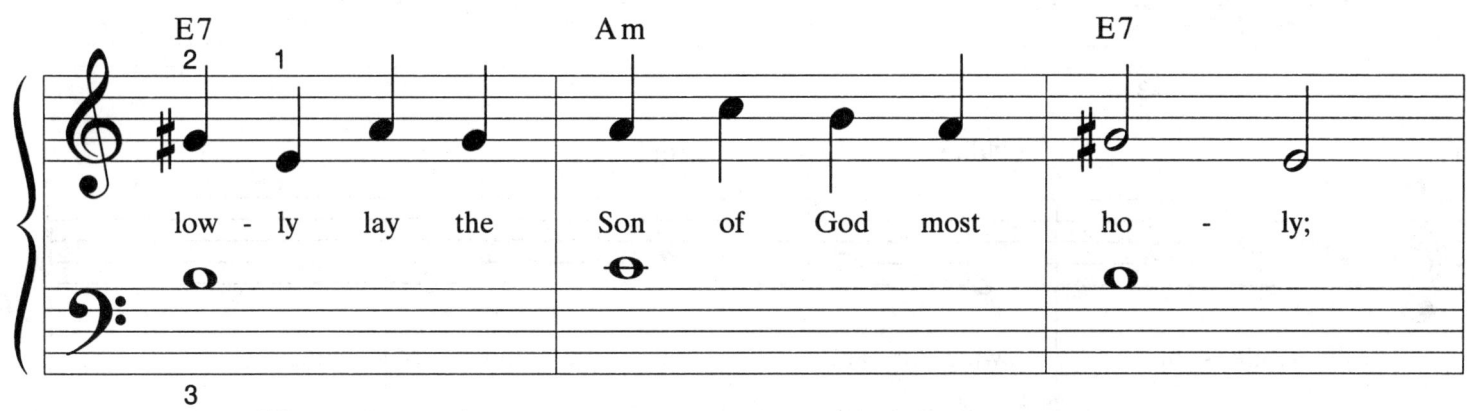

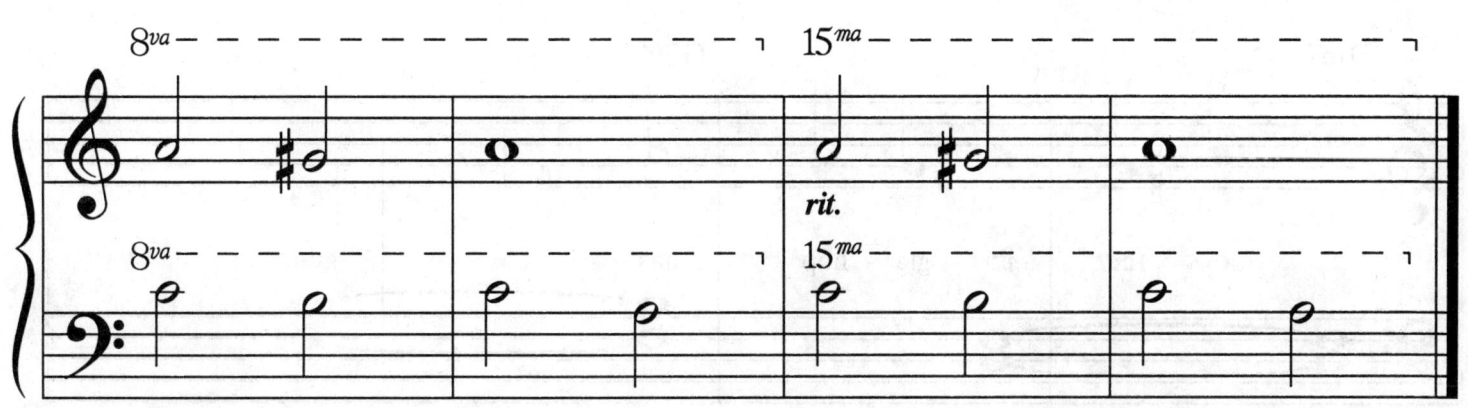

JINGLE-BELL ROCK

Words and Music by
JOE BEAL and JIM BOOTHE
Arranged by Richard Bradley

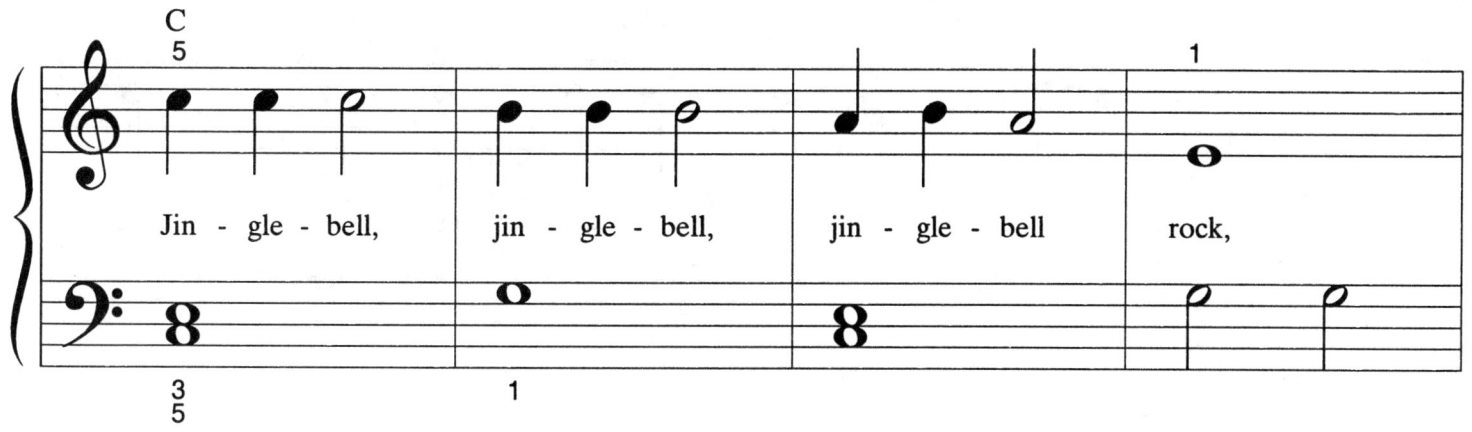
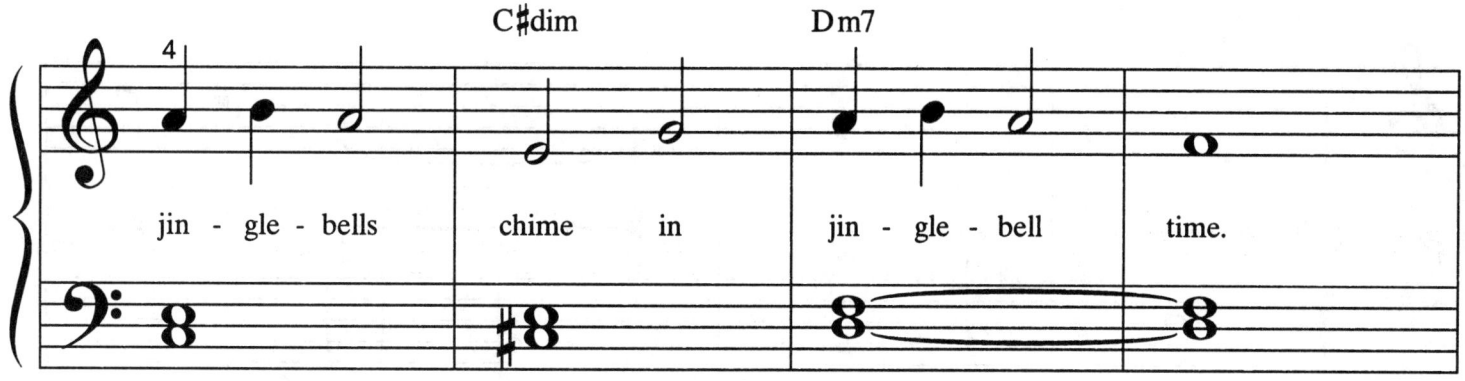
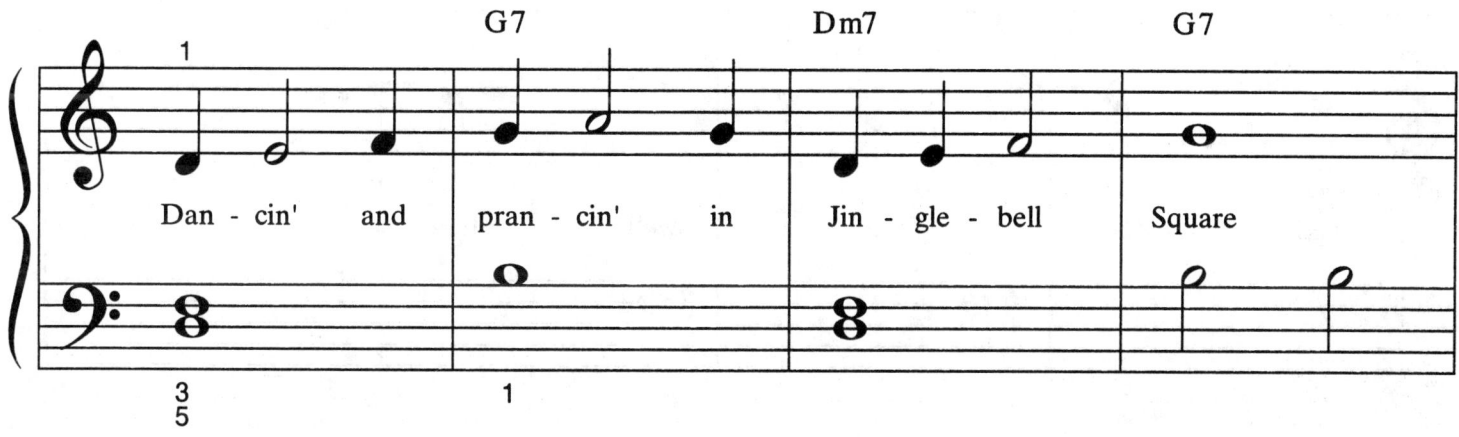
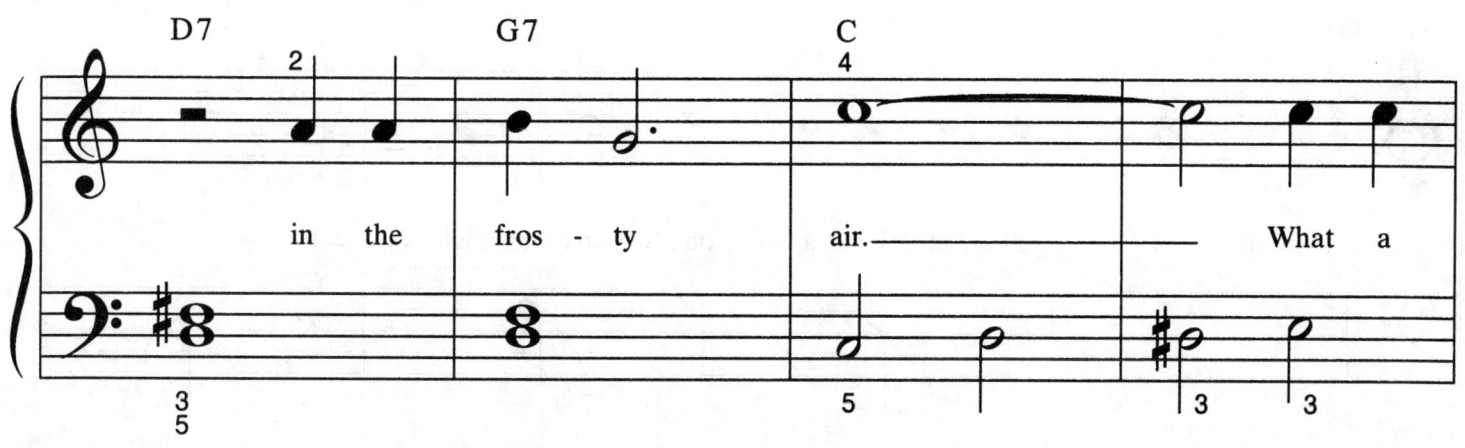

68

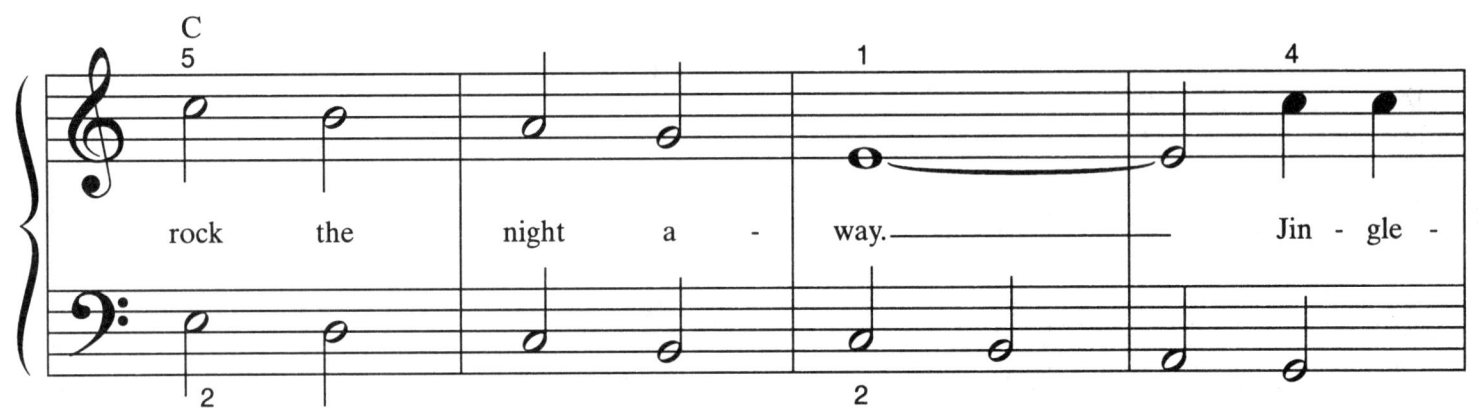

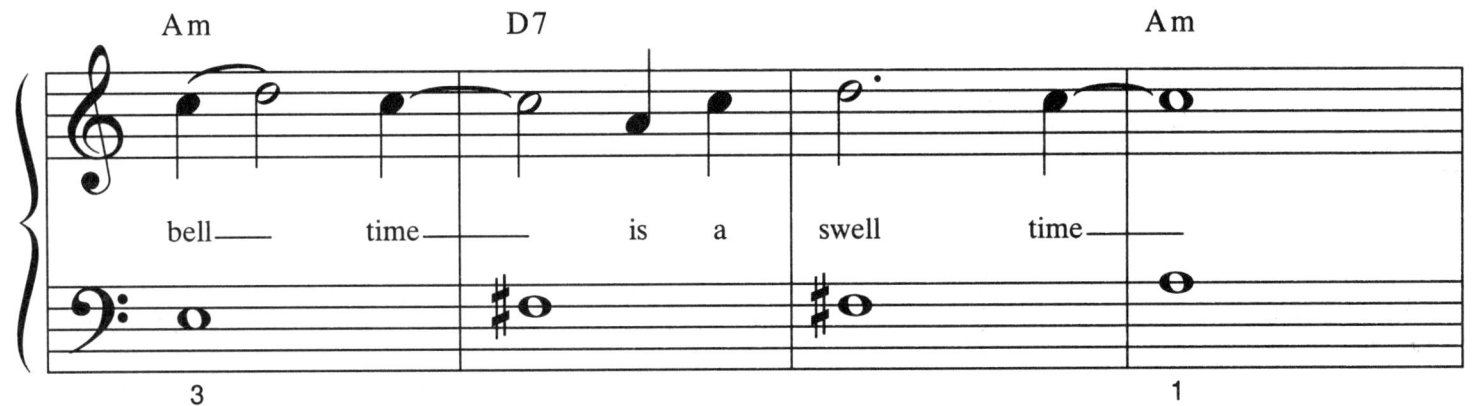

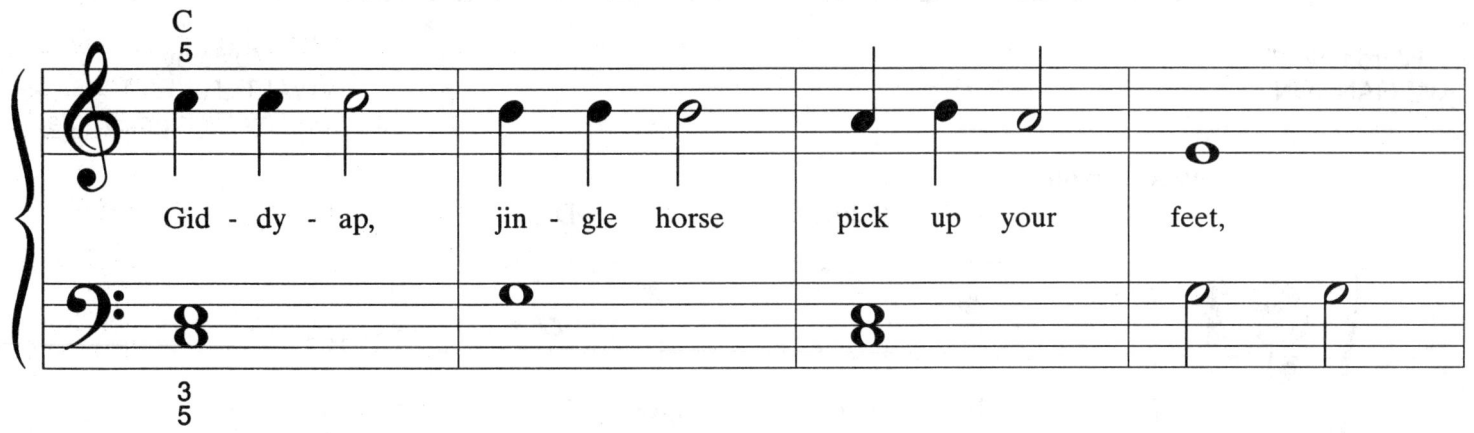
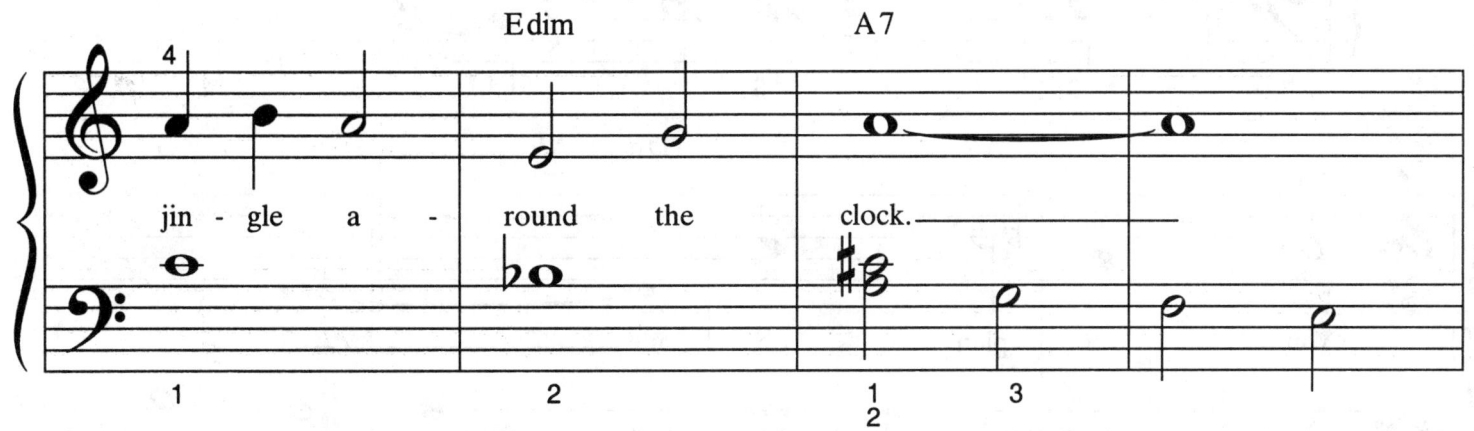

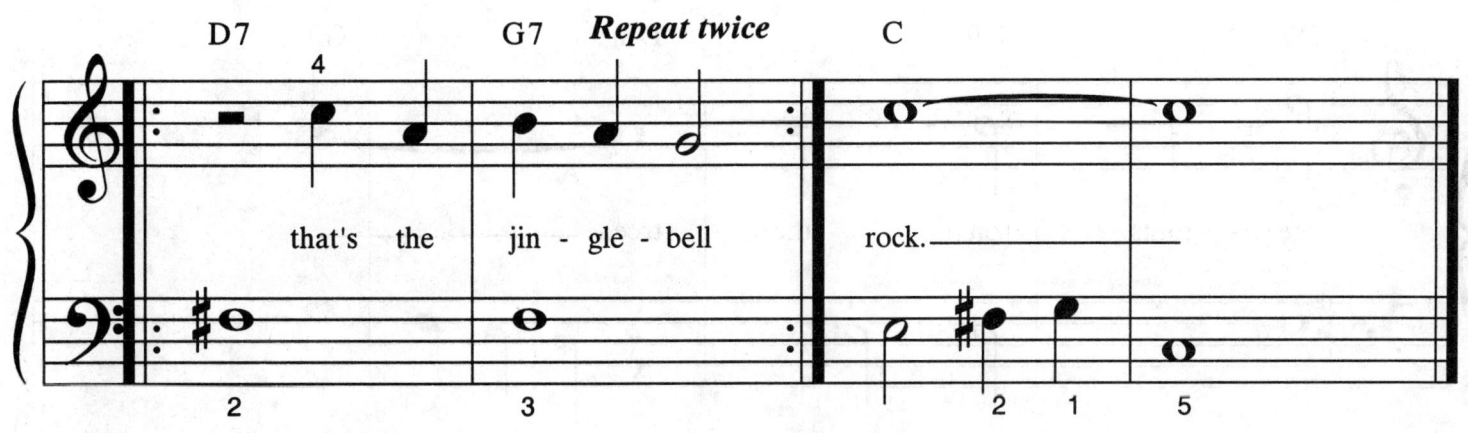

I'LL BE HOME FOR CHRISTMAS

Words by KIM GANNON

Music by WALTER KENT
Arranged by Richard Bradley

I'll Be Home for Christmas - 2 - 2

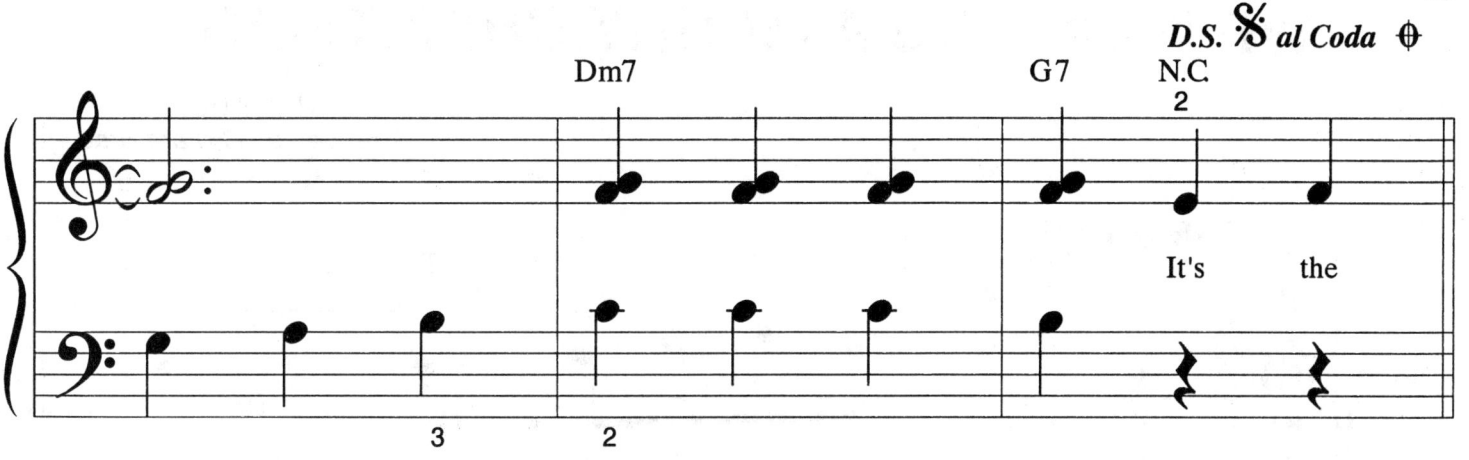
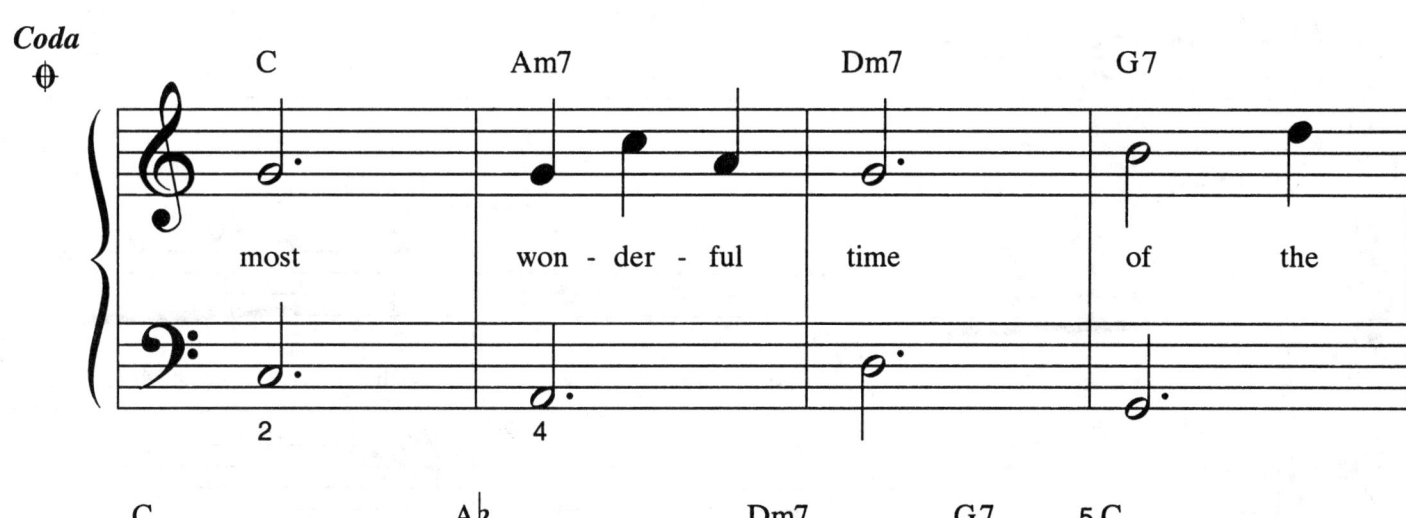

Verse 2:
It's the hap-happiest season of all.
With those holiday greetings,
And gay happy meetings
When friends come to call,
It's the hap-happiest season of all.

Verse 3:
It's the most wonderful time of the year.
There'll be much mistletoeing
And hearts will be glowing,
When loved ones are near.
It's the most wonderful time of the year.

77

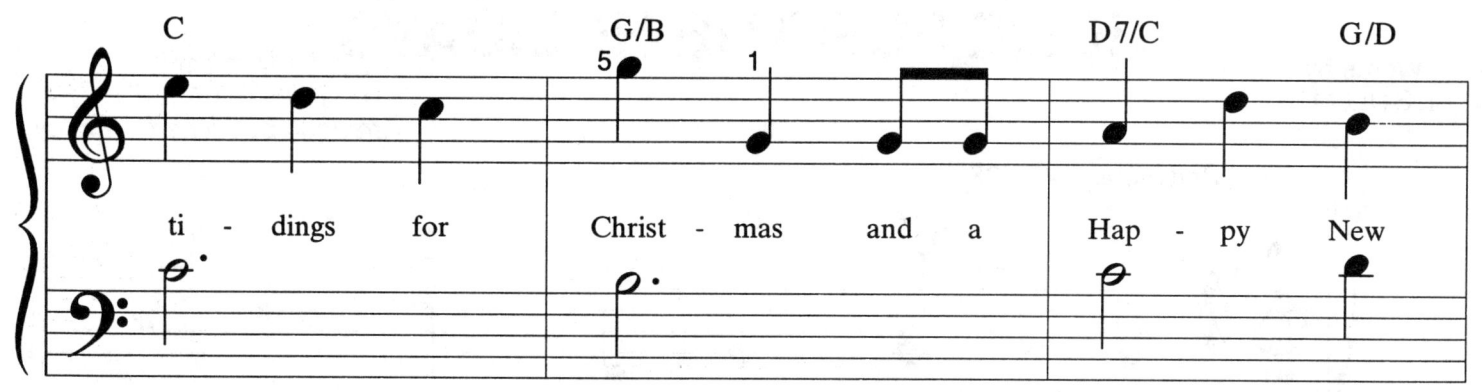

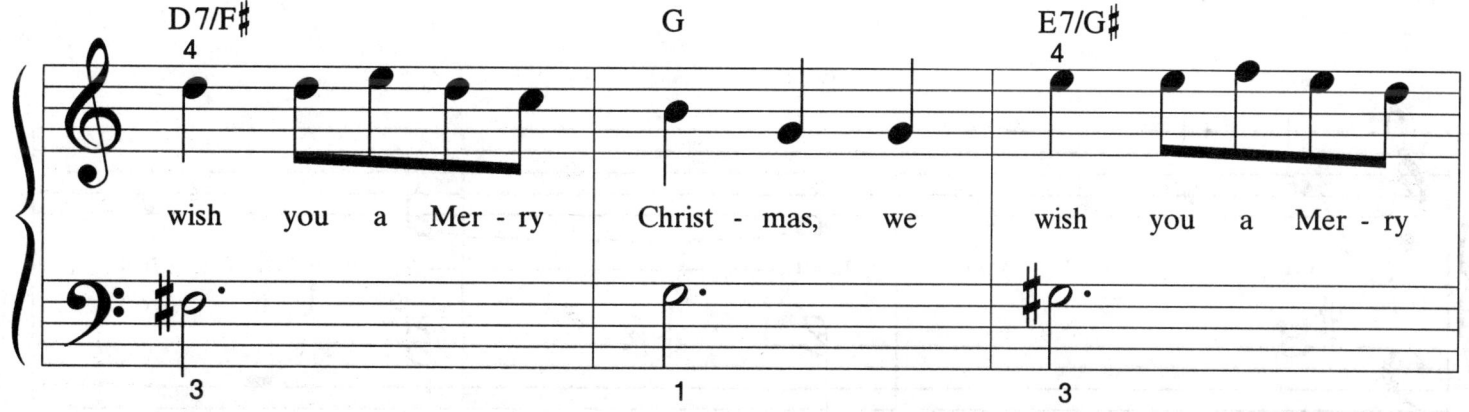
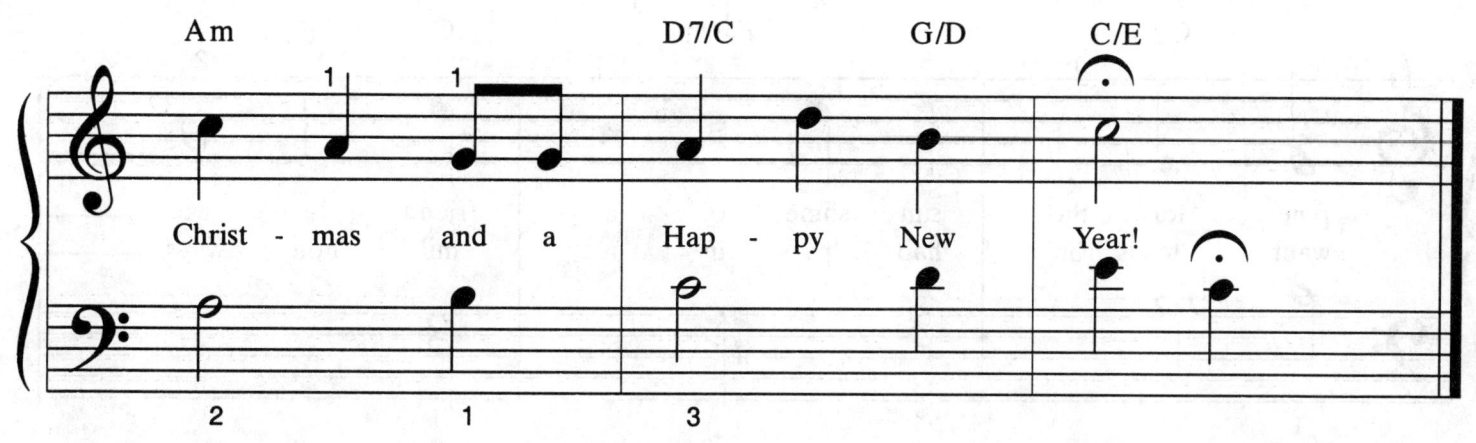

We Wish You a Merry Christmas - 2 - 2